JOURNEY
TO THE WHITE HOUSE

THROUGH A GLOBAL PANDEMIC

SALLY FOSTER

Copyright © Sally Foster 2021
This book is sold subject to the condition that it shall not, by way of trade or otherwise, be lent, resold, hired out, or otherwise circulated without the publisher's prior consent in any form of binding or cover other than that in which it is published and without a similar condition including this condition being imposed on the subsequent publisher.
The moral right of Sally Foster has been asserted.
ISBN-13: 9798536194171

*Dedicated to my husband Scott and our family,
for their love and support bringing light and inspiration to my life.*

ACKNOWLEDGEMENTS

My grateful thanks to the friends who supported and proofread for me sharing their knowledge and offering vital input.

CONTENTS

CREDITS i
PLAGIARISM STATEMENT v
PREFACE 1
CHAPTER 1 March Landscape 6
CHAPTER 2 Postponed Primaries – United States of America 11
CHAPTER 3 Wisconsin 14
CHAPTER 4 Growing Effects of the Pandemic on the Elections 18
CHAPTER 5 Responding to the Pandemic, Changing the Way We Work and Live 19
CHAPTER 6 President Trump and The World Health Organisation 25
CHAPTER 7 WHO Responds 27
CHAPTER 8 Delayed Democratic Primaries as of 21st April 2020 29
CHAPTER 9 Airtime – April 32
CHAPTER 10 Where Things Stand 33
CHAPTER 11 A Moving Tapestry – April into May 35
CHAPTER 12 The Making of a Vice-President 37
CHAPTER 13 Patchwork Reopening? 43
CHAPTER 14 The Vice President and Michelle Obama 51
CHAPTER 15 Campaigning Virtually 55
CHAPTER 16 Mail-in Voting in all Primaries – May 59
CHAPTER 17 As May Ends, Where Are We Now? 63
CHAPTER 18 Campaigning, Covid, and Cybercrime 70
CHAPTER 19 Campaigns and More Covid 76
CHAPTER 20 Primary Standings and the Way Forward 81
CHAPTER 21 President Trump's Finances, Supreme Court Rulings, and Roger Stone 86
CHAPTER 22 16 Weeks Until Election Day! 88
CHAPTER 23 Shifting Landscapes as Conventions Approach 93
CHAPTER 24 When Does a Campaign Begin? 99
CHAPTER 25 Changing Gear En Route To The White House 106
CHAPTER 26 Kamala Harris, Vice President 110
CHAPTER 27 Democratic National Convention – Virtual History 117
CHAPTER 28 The Republican National Convention, Unconventionally! 127
CHAPTER 29 Rolling into September as Biden Speaks Out Against Trump 138
CHAPTER 30 Week Two in September on the Campaign Trail 144
CHAPTER 31 Week Three in September 150

CHAPTER 32 Jostling for Position in the Polls 158
CHAPTER 33 Amy Coney Barrett 162
CHAPTER 34 When September Ends 164
CHAPTER 35 Trump Tests Positive for Coronavirus 169
CHAPTER 36 The Home Stretch and Turbulence 176
CHAPTER 37 Trump Trails 180
CHAPTER 38 The Final Countdown and Supreme Court Nomination 186
CHAPTER 39 The Vote! 195
CHAPTER 40 The Final Result 200
CHAPTER 41 Mr President Meets The First 100 Days! 203
CHAPTER 42 Thanksgiving on 26th November to December 3rd 212
CHAPTER 43 On to Christmas and Inauguration 215
CHAPTER 44 New Year, New Beginning, New President 223
CHAPTER 45 Happy New Year! 229
ABOUT THE AUTHOR 247

Credits

The main source of information, reports, and statistics both political and economic are taken from but not limited to The New York Times *daily brief,* On Politics and Coronavirus *updates via daily email alerts. Other media is also quoted and credited throughout including News Channels, Newspapers, online reporting, and a variety of publications. Any thoughts or opinions are, where appropriate, clearly noted as my own and not included as fact.*

Journalists credited from the following sources as footnotes throughout:

- ABC News, Mike Memoli
- Centre for Responsive Politics (Campaign fund figures)
- New York Times, references

Daily brief and On Politics by:

- Lisa Lerer
- Nicholas Fandos – Congressional correspondent, Washington
- Mark Makela
- Nicole Pelroth
- Matthew Roseberg
- Isabella Kwai
- Nick Corasaniti
- Shane Goldmacher
- Richard Faucet
- Reid J. Epstein
- Aimee Ortizo and Katharine Q Seelye

- Rick Rojas
- Nate Cohn
- Andrea Kannapell
- Giovanni Russonello
- Alexander Burns
- Maggie Astor
- Annie Karni, Astead W Herndon
- Matt Flegenheimer
- Shane Goldmacher and Maggie Haberman
- Alan Feuer and Luke Broadwater
- Michael Levenson and Emily Cochrane
- Victoria Shannon

The Washington Post:
- Annie Linskey
- Matt Visor
- *The Daily Show* with Trevor Noah

Further Sources:
- BBC News
- CNN. Eric Bradner and Gregory Krieg
- Castbox
- Matthew Syed, The Ping Pong Guy, Book- Rebel Ideas
- Wikipedia
- Google images
- Politico. NYT
- Fox News
- Vandana Rambaran
- On Politics NYT
- Maggie Matt and Stevens

- ABC News
- Stengle, Dallas and Weber
- Politico NYT
- Christopher Cadelago and Natasha Korechi
- *The Guardian*
- Katrina Manson, *Financial Times*, Washington
- Aishvarya Kavi

BBC North America reporter: Anthony Zurcher.

NYT Cyber extract: Mark Makela, Nicole Pelroth, David E. Sanger, Matthew Rosaberg.

Quote references:

- President Trump
- President Obama
- Former Vice President and Democratic Nominee Joe Biden
- Senator Kamala Harris
- Sean McElwee, co-founder of left leaning polling firm *Data for Progress*
- Dr Anthony Fauci
- Michael Michalko
- Adhanom Ghebreyesus, WHO Director General
- Dr Amesh Adalja, expert on infectious diseases
- Joseph Borrell, EU foreign policy chief
- Matt Rourke AP, Steven Sennel AP
- Max Whittaker, NYT
- Governor Michelle Lujan Grisham, New Mexico
- Chief Justice, Supreme Court, John G Roberts
- Mitt Romney, Republican senator
- Pat Toomeu, Republican senator

- ❏ Judge Charles W Dodson, Leon County Circuit Court
- ❏ Donald Trump Jr.

Further Citations

Pierre Somse, Central African Republic Health Minister. Jacinda Ardern, Prime Minister of New Zealand. Sergei Ryabkov, Russian deputy foreign minister. Scott Morrison, Prime Minister Australia. Chairman, US House of Representatives. Foreign Affairs Minister. Joseph Borrell.

Plagiarism Statement

The study was written by me by drawing on various media sources online, where my own words, thoughts, or any opinions are noted in italics. Quotations from published and unpublished sources are indicated in the footnotes and acknowledgements where appropriate. The source of any map, picture, or statistic is also indicated as is the source, published or unpublished, of any material drawn from multimedia sources in researching the events reported on.

PREFACE

A diary account of the Democratic Presidential Primaries and the subsequent campaign for the Presidential election 3rd November 2020. Including the emerging Covid-19 Pandemic, how it impacted on the aforementioned campaigns, as well as the effect on the world economy, employment, healthcare, social injustices, and climate change. A flavour of racial tensions erupting over the summer months of 2020 focusing on affairs in the US but with a seasoning of politics and evolving daily events from around the globe, including but not limited to the United Kingdom, Russia, China, and Europe.

An unprecedented chapter in American and world history led Joseph R Biden Jr to The White House and to the departure of President Donald Trump. The story is, I believe, fascinating, heart-breaking, and inspiring. From reports of incredible suffering to the despair of many in the early stages of the Pandemic to the real grind of living through it, particularly as America seeks to elect a new President and Britain navigates a bumpy course to Brexit and leaving the European Union, to eventual signs of hope with the development of a vaccine and the first days of populations receiving the first vaccinations. New ways of working, of persevering, of success for some and devastation from others. Finding kindness and courage in fellow human beings. Positive signs on the Global Climate brought about by huge changes in the way we live work and play. Most of all it is history in the making which all who read this today have lived through and for the generations to come after us it will hopefully give an insight into 2020, whichever country we live in. Writing from my home in Scotland I have been struck by the sheer enormity of the term 'Pandemic' which somehow makes me question how just one single word can describe the global situation. The position in

February 2020 leading up to March 11th when this full story to Inauguration Day 20th January 2021 begins tells us of news reports of the first stirrings of the Presidential campaign as the Democratic Primaries begin to gain momentum amid an emerging news story from China of a new virus. Coronavirus, thought to have originated from bats sold at live food markets in Wuhan which causes an illness called Covid-19. The illness attacks human lungs. There is no cure, there is no vaccine; highly contagious, it is a killer.

United States of America US Presidential Campaign 2020
Election date: 3rd November 2020
Who is running for President?

Donald Trump

Republican and incumbent and 45th President of the United States of America launches a re-election campaign for Republican Primaries. Some republican parties cancel their primaries in a show of support for Mr Trump.

Meanwhile, 29 major candidates launched campaigns for the Democratic Nomination which is the largest field for any party in the post-reform period of American politics. The campaign runs from the Presidential Primary elections from February to June 2020. Known as an indirect election, voters cast ballots selecting a slate of delegates to a party nominating convention who then in turn elect their nominee for President and Vice President.

In February four frontrunners emerged which forms the focus of the study of this journey to the White House and the election of the 46th President of the United States.

Bernie Sanders; 78, 08/09/1941 from Brooklyn, New York.

Pledged delegates: 46

Bernie Sanders served as junior Senator from Vermont since 2007 and as US representative for the state at large congressional districts from 1991 to 2007. In early March, Sanders won the North Dakota Democratic caucus. By Super Tuesday he is beginning to see Biden's support grow. He is hopeful of winning swing states like Michigan, which went to Biden. Some feel that Sanders could defeat Trump, but the reality is looking like he will not be the Democratic nominee.

Pete Buttigieg; 38, 19/01/1982 from South Bend, Indiana.

Pledged 26 delegates but subsequently dropped out of the bid on March 20th.

Joe Biden; 77, 20/11/1942 from Scranton, Pennsylvania. Former Vice President to Barack Obama.

Pledged delegates: 15

In early Primaries Biden fared well, winning in Idaho, Mississippi,

and Missouri. Also winning in Michigan which carried the largest delegate count on the line in this group at 125. In March in the so-called Super Tuesday primaries, Biden won some surprise victories and eked out the delegate pledge over Sanders. At this point Tulsi Gabbard is still in the race but the contest is shaping up to be between Biden and Sanders. Pete Buttigieg, as mentioned above, drops out of the race and throws support behind Joe Biden.

Elizabeth Warren; 70, 22/06/1949, from Oklahoma City, Oklahoma.

Pledged eight delegates but subsequently dropped out of the bid on March 20th before Super Tuesday. In dropping out of the race it was thought unlikely she would endorse Sanders even although they agree on some progressive issues. A rift in political coalitions hinted that she did not believe Sanders could win. Even so many of her staffers (maybe 40) endorsed Sanders and she pledged to stay in the fight for US Democrats.

CHAPTER 1

March Landscape

Avidly reading various reports online, in the newspapers and across various news channels in the UK and some snapshots from the US, it is my understanding that by early March only two real contenders for the Presidential nomination are evident. Conclusions drawn from political writers indicate that Super Tuesday was not good for Sanders as Biden swept through to multiple victories. Sanders had expected perhaps to be saved by a surge of young voters and blue-collar votes. We begin to see differences emerge where Sanders polled ahead of Biden among white and young Americans without college educations but could not overcome the vote for Biden from older, moderate, possibly suburban white voters and his popularity among older African American voters. Sanders now looks to mitigate his losses and prioritises the mid-Western states and seeking African American votes. Attacks on Biden's record, media and the Democratic establishment all failed to bring the votes Sanders craved. It begins to look like Biden will win the nomination, but it is widely thought that in order to defeat President Trump he will need support from the Sanders voters. I am just beginning to pick up this story and I have a lot to learn but I am able to note from the reports this week that the swing states for 2020 are thought to be, based on trends for 2012 to 2016, Arizona, Florida, Maine, Michigan, Minnesota, Nebraska's 2nd congressional district, New Hampshire, North Carolina, Pennsylvania, and Wisconsin. Swing states are targeted by both Republican and Democratic parties *while they may assume safe states have sufficient support. They will hold the key to victory, I think, for candidates. Notably, I learn that swing states previously held by Obama which Trump won in 2016 include Michigan, Pennsylvania, Wisconsin, Florida, Ohio, and Idaho. Primaries continue with Biden doing well with wins in Idaho, Maine, Minnesota, Texas, and North Carolina while Sanders wins in New Hampshire and California. Later, in March, Biden won in Illinois, Florida, and Arizona.*

It is around this point that the Coronavirus begins to impact the Democratic Primary process. Ohio postpones their Primary. At this point in mid-March Joe Biden has 1153 pledged delegates. Bernie Sanders has 861. 1991 pledged delegates are required to win, and it is looking like Bernie Sanders cannot catch Joe Biden. As I read the news updates from various media sources in the US and at home, I am feeling a growing sense of unease as 'the virus' is getting ever closer to our shores and I am actually wondering how and when the UK government will take swift action to protect us all.

The Black Vote, 18th March 2020

Focussing the bulk of my quest for knowledge and news on the New York Times *while reading various other news websites, I am able to follow the results from the Democratic Primaries and as I write I try to learn more about each State as I go along and in particular where each candidate seems to be most popular. Joe Biden seems to appeal to a block of southern voters Bernie Sanders cannot reach. On Super Tuesday Joe Biden's largest wins came in largely black voter states such as Virginia, Alabama, North Carolina, and Arkansas. He won 10 from 14 states, taking almost two thirds of the black votes. Biden has won the most black votes in every state like the Democratic nominees of the past 30 years with just one exception in John Kerry 2004 who finished three points behind John Edwards in only one state.*

There is so much to learn, not just about the system of choosing a Democratic Presidential Candidate but about the different States and the diversity of the whole country. Living in Scotland's capital city of Edinburgh in the United Kingdom I suddenly feel we are such a small island. Anyway, to continue I learn that Southern black voters appear to shape or change the course of the Democratic primaries and can influence who wins the race to the White House. Over five decades black voters have supported the Democratic candidate and votes are concentrated in the south where most states vote Republican. However, in the so-called "swing states" the black vote could be a deciding factor. Where Sanders, Warren, and Bloomberg fail to reach the black voters Biden seems to do well. All the reporters I am following are thorough and knowledgeable and seem to thrive on their work I feel.

In response to this atmosphere President Trump and his Republican campaigners, who are aware of this, have started a "Black voices for Trump" initiative in Atlanta. In his State of the Union address he reached out to "bootstrapping black Americans" and announced plans to open community centres targeting black communities in seven key battleground states. Black voter support for Republicans averaged in 1968 to 2004 around 11 percent. In the Trump era of 2016 it is thought to be around 8%. Biden's Super Tuesday results point at a closer contest than Trump would like or have anticipated perhaps. A month ago (February 2020) Biden looked an unlikely challenger but now is emerging as the frontrunner nominee and as a possible challenge. The more people who vote the better it will be for Joe Biden.

Coronavirus Arrives

A historical moment in the year; the Coronavirus outbreak which began, as far as we are told, from a live animal market, specifically in relation to bats in the Chinese district of Wuhan, begins to dominate news around the world. The outbreak quickly leaps to Europe as people travel out of China. Much more on this follows in the coming months but for now the focus is in and around Italy and Spain. The United Kingdom, having hosted fairly large sporting events with people travelling from Europe, is fast becoming a hub of Coronavirus cases as is the United States of America, particularly New York. Records show that governments around the world are struggling to contain, to control, and to act quick enough to avoid what quickly moves from an outbreak to an epidemic to a pandemic. By late March, "lockdown" closes the world.

This is really where my study of what was initially just looking at the Democratic Primaries in the United States of America evolves into a chapter in all our histories, the likes of which no living person has ever seen before. By 23rd March, in Scotland where I live, full lockdown of all four nations of the United Kingdom are put in place and we are to stay at home and only leave for exercise once per day locally, to shop for essential food or medicine, to care for a dependant or to go to work. Key workers are given letters to authorize their movements. Those over 70 or with underlying health conditions (of which I am one of) must shield completely as they are considered high risk if they contract Coronavirus which causes the lethal Covid-19 illness so cannot leave their home at all. I am afraid, I am anxious, and now facing the unknown alongside my husband and daughter at home with me. We have two sons, both living 40 miles away in opposite directions. My elderly and very ill mother is 40 miles away and although supported by carers, is at very high risk. In the words made famous by a fictional US President in the year 2000 in The West Wing; *"What's next?"*[1]

Similar restrictions to the UK are in place around the globe, as the United States of America travels headlong into the crisis in Presidential election year. Month by month I will track what happens next. I will continue to draw from any and all reporting

---

[1] Creator: Aaron Sorkin.

although I think the more technical and contentious the situation becomes, I may have to limit my scope to a smaller group of media. See where the journey leads me, I think.

CHAPTER 2

Postponed Primaries –

United States of America

April Landscape

Just as March is drawing to a close, eleven states have announced they will postpone their Democratic primaries as Coronavirus cases rise, deaths rise, jobs are lost, and the economy begins to flounder. Of those states postponing decisions are quickly made to move to mail-in votes while the Democratic National Committee (DNC) indicates it will continue to plan to hold the convention July 13th-16th. Early statistics gathered show in the US 46,450 cases of the virus and at least 595 deaths. As the Pandemic escalates it is thought the peak is two to three weeks away as of 29th March 2020.

> *Here at home the health crisis is literally worsening by the day. The news channels are reporting alarming statistics and the pictures from around the world, particularly Italy, are so scary. The virus is very fast moving and very infectious. Feeling a little afraid already at the pace of the crisis at home but having set myself the challenge of writing up what I learn about the Democratic Primaries it feels right to continue, and not panic at what is unfolding. Hopefully, we get on top of the situation swiftly. Lockdown! Even the word feels strange having always been fortunate to live with full freedoms to choose how I live, work, and play.*

As April begins the position after the early primaries is:

Joe Biden – 1,217 pledged delegates. Bernie Sanders – 914 pledged delegates.

A candidate must secure 1,991 pledged delegates to win the nomination.

The problems arising from postponing primaries as the Pandemic grows need now to be looked at and quickly. Practical and legal matters need to be addressed as well as mitigating risk of spreading the virus through the primaries. The US begins to look at strategies to mitigate risk, including –

1. reviewing their States' continuity of government.
2. constitutional provisions.
3. continuity of legislatures during emergency plans.
4. election emergency statutes.
5. contingency plans at State and local levels.

Much of the above responsibilities lie with local jurisdictions or the executive branch. Legislation is being introduced to address how elections can be well executed as public gatherings are discouraged.

Policy options could be to delay or reschedule elections. Relocate polling stations. In most States, Governors have authority to do so but under general emergency heading they could action such options, including changing the date. Worth noting here that;

- Some states request or require that local election authorities provide contingency plans. Chief election officers may provide guidance to local authorities.
- There is a list in most states of who can be an "absentee" postal voter. Legislation would need to be in place to allow for "self-isolating" to be a reason. Public health risk could and should be added.
- Where polling places are allocated in long-term care facilities, they could potentially be moved. Usually, two to three months' notice is required but this could be actioned under emergency

law. President Trump has by this point declared a "State of Emergency".

- Review provisional ballot laws. If a voter can get to an alternative location, will the vote count?
- Poll workers may not be willing to work due to the risk attached. Communal stations where more than one precinct votes, a vote centre may be an option and reduce the number of poll workers needed.
- In many States people with disabilities have an option to use kerbside voting. An officer brings a ballot paper to the car. This option could be extended. Legislatures are currently responding to the Coronavirus pandemic and its effect on the elections with three bills. Either pending or enacted in three categories as follows:

Delaying elections; - Alabama, Massachusetts, New York, Pennsylvania.

Absentee/mail-in ballot; - Alaska, Louisiana, New York, Ohio, Pennsylvania.

Public health; - Colorado, Kentucky, New Jersey, New York.

Executive Action

In addition, States are using executive action to adjust elections in response to the Coronavirus which causes the illness known as Covid-19. By 1st April 2020, executive actions pertaining to public health have been raised by North Carolina 12/03, Louisiana 13/03, Georgia 14/03, Colorado 16/03, Kentucky 16/03, Ohio 16/03, Maryland 17/03, Alabama 18/03, Missouri 18/03, Oklahoma 18/03, Texas 18/03, Connecticut 19/03, New Jersey 19/03, Indiana 20/03, Mississippi 20/03, Rhode Island 23/03, Delaware 24/03, New York 28/03 [2].

---

[2] National Conference of State Legislatures

CHAPTER 3

Wisconsin

By 6th April it is noted that the Puerto Rico Primary is delayed until 26th April and with just two delegates running; Joe Biden and Bernie Sanders.

However, one day earlier on 5th April, Republicans in Wisconsin rebuffed the bid to delay the primary. So, it will go ahead on April 7th. It will be an in-person election and will include the State's democratic primary and also a vote on State Supreme Court Justice. Wisconsin has more than 2,000 confirmed cases of Coronavirus (April 5th, 2020), and is the only state so far not to postpone or significantly change the process. The Republicans accused Wisconsin Governor Tony Evers of trying to undermine the election process. This, in spite of the existing "stay at home" order. It is thought by some that the Republicans are playing politics with people's health who must choose between taking a risk and voting or not voting and risking a very compromised result. There may not be enough workers to man the polling stations. So, the Governor ordered the National Guard to step in, but this is still not enough probably. Governor Evers could ask a health official to delay the primary, but this is unlikely to work. Such a move could prompt legal challenges which could impact on future powers. Governor Evers seems locked in a political struggle with the Republicans.

Wisconsin Primary

The primary went ahead on 7th April although results are not due until 13th April. But what actually happened on the day? The electoral system appeared stretched to its very limits as people weighed up whether to risk their health and vote or stay home out of fears of the safety of voting amid the growing crisis. Long lines of people gathered even before voting began. Many, if not all, wore masks or face coverings and even some officials wore Hazmat suits. With the democratic presidential primary to be decided and the vote for the State Supreme Court seat to be decided, Wisconsin people voted in their thousands. The normal number of polling stations in Milwaukee were reduced from 180 to just five. While some waited in line for up to two hours others voted kerb side and polling stations in other locations were also used. Milwaukee has the biggest minority population in the state. In Wisconsin, with the system stretched, the political institutions proved over matched with a Republican legislature, a conservative state, and federal judiciary resisting efforts to reschedule or revise the procedure for voting.

Wisconsin: Before the Results are Known. Bernie Sanders news 8th April

Bernie Sanders announces that he can see no way of gaining enough votes to beat Joe Biden to the nomination. He announces his withdrawal from the bid. Sanders throughout his bid has focused on healthcare and income equality as his key issues. Also campaigning for free public college, raising taxes on the wealthy, and increasing minimum wage. In 2016, Sanders bid for the nomination failed as he lost out to Hillary Clinton. But in both campaigns he found favour with younger voters. He also garnered support from celebrities such as Cardi B, Arianna Grande, Miley

Cyrus to name but a few. His early and promising successes however gave way to Joe Biden as he swept through Texas, North Carolina, in early March, then Florida, Arizona, and Illinois. Biden appears to draw an African American vote which Sanders cannot reach. Therefore, Joe Biden, aged 77, is now expected to be crowned Democrat nominee at the convention scheduled for August. He will then face President Trump in the campaign for President of the United States of America.

Sanders concluded that while he could not win he believes his ideology contributed to change in American consciousness as to what kind of nation it could become and that he had helped take the country forward in the struggle for economic and social justice, racial justice, and environmental justice. He believes in influencing the younger voters, having gained favour from the 30 and underage group as well as the 50 and underage group. He congratulated Joe Biden on his expected success and pledged to continue to work with him to further the Democrat cause. Even although not campaigning, Sanders wishes to remain on ballot papers to gather delegates who can have an input on the party platform at the convention. He stands firm in his belief that the Democratic party can triumph over Trump.

Sanders withdrawal from the race came about perhaps as a direct result of the Coronavirus pandemic. He was forced to campaign remotely by video link from his home in Vermont. Hopes of a comeback derailed by delayed primaries and more damaging the cancellation of all public events and public gatherings. His early successes armed with support, backed by money, and gaining momentum really looked like he would win the nomination but his failure to do so will perhaps be written in history as a direct result of the pandemic. But, at 78, as his life as a public figure draws to a close, possibly his success in pushing the party to the left on healthcare, equality, and college fees will be counted as a positive from many.

Joe Biden Responds to Bernie Sanders Withdrawal

Joe Biden responded to Sanders' withdrawal by hailing him a good man, a great leader, and a powerful voice for change. He was thankful for Sanders putting American people first and would reach out to him and ensure both their voices are heard. Also, more tellingly he reaches out to Sanders' supporters. He will need their support if he is to defeat Trump in November. Meanwhile, President Trump responds by questioning why Joe Biden has not been supported by President Obama, who he served under as vice-president. This aside, 100% focus is on the growing pandemic and few will want to detract from this.

CHAPTER 4

Growing Effects of the Pandemic on the Elections

The Democratic National Convention (DNC) has now, as a direct result of delayed primaries and events due to Coronavirus, had to push back the planned convention to week beginning 17th August and will take place in Milwaukee, Wisconsin. It has never been hosted in this battleground state in the Midwest before.

The Wisconsin Primary Result

Joe Biden, 58 pledged delegates. Bernie Sanders, 13 pledged delegates.

With Sanders now out of the race but remaining on the ballot he has endorsed Joe Biden, so the result is as expected. With the Democratic convention scheduled for 17th August as noted previously, the scheduled Republican convention is set to begin 24th August. It is expected President Trump will be formally declared the Republican candidate for President. No change to this date has been suggested so far (April 13th).

CHAPTER 5

Responding to the Pandemic, Changing the Way We Work and Live

By mid-April 2020 it is clear that the virus is here to stay, not just in the USA but around the world. The situation at home is very worrying on every level from public health crisis to economy, jobs, and just about every other issue facing society. Fear, alarm, and distress is becoming a part of life from waking up in the morning to closing my eyes at night. Scientists from around the world are working at unprecedented speed to find a vaccine, starting trials as soon as possible.

In the US, the virus is ripping through the southern states, devastating the African American community's life and the road back to "normal" is increasingly further away. Evidently, like it or not we all have to find a way of living with it. No vaccine, no cure, and all affected countries are in lockdown. This is truly awful.

In Wuhan where the virus originated, or so it is thought, strict lockdown and quarantine measures are in place. Italy, Spain, and the UK are by now hotspots. What does lockdown mean? Well, each country has different methods but essentially the world is closing. In Scotland (where I live) all shops are closed except for food and medicine. All pubs, bars, and restaurants are closed. The tourism and hospitality industries are closed. Many can only leave their homes for essential food and medicine. Transport network is running at minimal capacity only to facilitate transport for "key workers." Key workers are those who work in food and medical areas, government, transport, emergency services, care services. Schools, colleges, universities are all closed. Industry and manufacturing stops. Car sales and manufacturing stops. Offices, libraries, post offices are closed. Banks are closed except in the UK where branches remain open on minimum staff for shorter hours. We, like many around Europe, are told to stay at home, only essential travel allowed and no contact with other households at all. I can't fully comprehend how this has happened in 2020 and I look at my three grown up children, seeing the effect this is having on them as the life they knew has been suspended and we all cling on to hope that it will be over soon. We are a long way from that hope becoming reality.

While we all start to try and reconcile what is happening as we lose our freedom, our choice, our social contact with our loved ones, friends, and colleagues, a change in the way we live and work emerges which would have been unthinkable even a few weeks ago. Essentially business and life must find a way to go forward. The number of Coronavirus cases around the world has not even reached the peak, millions are infected, and thousands are dying. This is an unprecedented time. How is it possible in 2020 with the knowledge, science, money, and resources from the world's superpowers that a virus, thought to have come from bats sold in an open-air market of live animals in Wuhan, China, has spread through the world and we have no cure, no vaccine? Human-to-human transmission through inhaling moisture droplets from an infected person and touching an infected surface are the two key ways the virus is spreading. So, all public gatherings and events are cancelled. "Social-distancing" is introduced. We must stay two metres away from everyone at all times (except those we live with). We must wear face coverings outside. We must wash our hands with soap for at least 20 seconds or use a hand sanitiser. The soap can collapse the cells of the virus. If you touch an infected surface then touch your eyes, nose, or mouth with infected hands you may get the virus. The virus will start with a dry persistent cough, a fever, and then difficulty breathing as it attacks *your lungs. Fear begins to take over our psyche. Writing is becoming more necessary for me as in addition to reading about the election I am reading so much now relating to the virus. It is not going to be as short lived as everyone hoped. The impact is being felt and everything is changing.*

Living with Covid-19 and Changing How We Live – April

An upside-down world and the good that can come from it is not something many of us looked into, however a few years ago Michael Michalko, a former US army officer, came up with a fascinating idea to sharpen creativity. [3]

He called it "assumption reversal".

Take the core notion of any concept then turn it on its head. For example, if you are starting a restaurant then the first assumption is that restaurants have menus. The reversal of course is "restaurants have no menus." Thought provoking and led to the idea that the chef tells you what he bought that day, and you select a customised dish. This may not be entirely workable, but it does lead to new innovations and workable schemes. It could be said that the virus caused us all to look for workable solutions to the problems it presents. Another example could be "taxi firms' own cars." Today though, Uber is a taxi firm, but the firm does not own cars. The point of this is that we are living through disruption which could be called a reversal with worldwide lives and businesses turned upside down.

---

[3] Michael Michalko

Opportunities amid darkness

Reversal techniques are typically used in creative industries, but can we seek out silver linings for ourselves? Are innovations inspired by the pandemic? Undoubtedly yes. If we look at Education it is typically delivered in classes in buildings to deliver facts. To reverse this is to say education is not about imparting knowledge. Provoking a response which leads to the idea of helping children develop skills not drawn from traditional disciplines and not on the curriculum. An example of this could be improvisation, working together, and learning on our feet in changing times.

Example for parents/carers

Leave a subject card face down in a room and ask the child to pick it up. Say for example the child is seven years old and the card is a picture of Paddington Bear, ask the child to speak for 60 seconds on the subject. She or he may fail at first but could be inspired to improvise or seek out the information required to speak with knowledge so leading to growing self-confidence and sense of achievement. Ask him or her to note down how they felt at first attempt and after hitting the goal. Learning comes in many forms. The key here is shifting a negative experience to a positive outcome.

Applying the principle to other platforms

The principle is easily applied to other areas including business. "Lawyers have offices." In current times lawyers are working from home, using technology to communicate and facilitate meetings with many people around the world. Documents can be prepared, emailed, scanned, signed, and registered all in the comfort of a lawyer's own home for example. Cost savings are huge in terms of travel before you even look at the cost saved if buildings were not required in the same quantity going forward. A further upside is easing congestion from the reduction in travel, easing pollution around the world, and all the while producing a more effective, less stressed workforce.

Kindness

In the UK as the crisis deepened over 700,000 people stepped up to offer help to the National Health Service. Can this kindness in whatever shape or form it comes be a permanent part of society or is it just in times of crisis people change? If we look at a study done of 600 medical students the findings are thought provoking. It was noted that selfish students who focused on themselves performed well in first year. They were "takers" and gave nothing in return. No kindness. Those more generous with their time and willing to help others – showing kindness – got left behind! But, curiously, by second year the cohorts had caught up. By third year they had overtaken their peers and by their final year the givers had significantly higher grades. It seems a kinder approach was a more powerful guide of final grades than knowledge of whatever the subject. The givers had not changed but the structure of the programme had and as they moved from class in first year to clinical and practical rotations and patient care success came as it was largely dependent on teamwork and service. Takers may win when knowledge is all that is required but people with a giving attitude thrive in interdependence situations. Givers, it could be said, are strategic, seeking out diversity but drawing away from people who seek only to exploit them. A world with more kindness and creativity is one to hope for and look forward to. Reaching out for solutions and leaving old ways and practices behind could lead us to light out of all this darkness. From an eminent scientist, "according to conventional wisdom, highly successful people have three things in common: -

Motivation

Ability

Opportunity."

But a fourth ingredient depends largely on how we approach our interactions with other people. Do we claim value for ourselves or do we add value? Simple choice, huge consequences for success.[4]

Matthew Syed is a Sunday Times (UK) author and columnist, co-host of BBC Podcast *Flintoff, Savage, and The Ping Pong Guy*. He is also co-founder of Greenhouse charity empowering youngsters through sport. A member of FA's technical advisory board and an ambassador for Pixl educational foundation.

---

[4] Matthew Syed author 'Rebel Ideas', 'The Power of Diverse Thinking.'

CHAPTER 6

President Trump and The World Health Organisation

April

Following on from a lot of noise from President Trump regarding the World Health Organisation, President Trump announces he will suspend funds going to the WHO from the USA. The Geneva-based organisation is accused by Trump of mishandling the Coronavirus outbreak and not acting quickly enough or openly enough to prevent it growing from an outbreak to an epidemic to a pandemic.

The following timeline guides us through to the announcement mid-April (15th)

Timeline:

January 30th – WHO issues travel guidance after reportedly saying earlier it is not needed.

January 31st – President Trump blocks travel from China, except for US citizens, residents, spouses, and family of US nationals. The Chinese government and the WHO condemn him.

March 13th – President Trump declares a national emergency. He grants 50 billion dollars in funding for US states and territories.

March 24th – Trump declares the US can open by April 12th and is warned against this by all.

April 7th – President Trump threatens to freeze WHO funding as the US death toll passes China's. He has missed a memo warning of mass deaths from Covid-19, the illness caused by Coronavirus. He blames the WHO for being China-centric. He blames the WHO for being slow to advise closing borders and was enraged at US funding being, in his opinion, mishandled.

April 8th – WHO officials deny his allegations while President Trump continues his attacks. The WHO's director-general Tedros Adhanon Gheyreyesus urges world leaders not to politicise the situation and Trump accuses the WHO of minimising the Covid-19 outbreak and of siding with China.

April 14th – Trump cuts the United States funding and funds are temporarily halted. He said the WHO "failed in its basic duty and it must be held accountable." He went on to say they promoted "disinformation about the virus which likely led to a greater outbreak." The WHO called for greater solidarity.

At this time, the number of people dying from Covid-19 in the US rose by at least 2,228 on Tuesday 14th April to exceed 28,300 deaths and cases reported as standing at around 600,000.

I learn from the media reports that this is three times more than any other country. The IMF (International Monetary Fund) expects the global economy to shrink by three per cent this year, representing the biggest contraction since The Great Depression of the 1930s.

Worldwide 1.98 million people are confirmed to have the virus. 126,500 have died and many hundreds of thousands of people, who have not been tested, will have had the virus. It is thought, although statistics vary from country to country, that around 486,500 will have recovered.

CHAPTER 7

WHO Responds

The centre for disease control said on April 15th that 19 to 20 US States may be ready to reopen. There are a number of counties without confirmed cases of Covid-19. At the same time the WHO announces their focus on saving lives and is critical of President Trump's decision to halt funding. World leaders fear he has taken a "dangerous step in the wrong direction." The US is the WHO's main contributor and stood at $400 million in 2019. President Trump continues to blame them for inaction leading to the catastrophic situation around the world.

Further Reactions to President Trump's Actions

The director general of the WHO, Adhanom Ghebreyesus, said "this is a time for us all to be united in our common struggle against a common threat … when we are divided the virus exploits the cracks between us." He vowed the WHO will continue its fight "without fear or favours." An early and important finding of fact is that the earlier all cases are found, tested, and isolated the harder it is for the virus to spread. He called for unity around the world and to all follow this principle which will save lives and mitigate the economic impact the world over as a result.

An expert on infectious diseases, Dr Amesh Adalja, admitted that the WHO made mistakes in the Ebola outbreak in West Africa in 2013/14 and that reform must take place after this crisis is over.

He encouraged all countries to work together and share information, knowledge, and to work towards opening borders.

European foreign policy chief, Joseph Borrell, said the 27-nation bloc "deeply regrets" President Trump's suspension of funds and that the health agency needs funds more than ever just now.

The CDC directs requests for comment directly to The White House.

President of the American Medical Association Patrice Harris called it "a dangerous step in the wrong direction" which will hinder defeating Covid-19 and urges Trump to reconsider.

Other figures expressing regret and keen for him to reconsider include; African Union head, Moussa Fakimahamat, Vanderbilt University Medical Centre, Central African Republic health minister Pierre Somse, Chairman US House of Representatives Foreign Affairs Minister, New Zealand Prime Minister Jacinda Ardern, Russian deputy Foreign Minister Sergei Ryabkov, and Australian Prime Minister Scott Morrison.

President Trump meets resistance as he continues to urge States to reopen as the decision for that lies with the Governors of each individual state. Data from 11th April shows that the US has purged 22 million jobs since mid-March. Shops, bars, restaurants, and the hospitality sector have closed doors. As this is happening the US defence secretary from The Pentagon, Mark Esper, is of the opinion that China's leaders have been misleading the world about Coronavirus from the beginning and does not feel that they can be trusted, he told NBC's Today programme.

CHAPTER 8

Delayed Democratic Primaries as of 21st April 2020

By April 21st, many primaries have been delayed, as is the DNC convention, however the party announces that no primaries can be held after June 9th. Due to Covid-19 and the continuing move to hold mail-in ballots and avoid in-person voting, many states ignore this guidance. New York delays until June 23rd even as this could result in losing delegates at the August convention. There are at this moment more than a dozen States in this position and trying to balance the public health risk against losing votes. The Democratic National Committee mandates that primaries held after June 9th will lose 50% of their delegates. New York Governor Andrew Cuomo holds firm that it is not safe to go ahead on the original date as New York is becoming the worst hit State. The rules also stated with regard to late primaries that "any candidate campaigning in a State with a contest outside of the designated calendar will not be awarded any delegates from that state … Campaigning is inclusive of print, internet use, phone calls." An extensive list which is inclusive "but not limited to" all those stated. Effectively, while not campaigning in person Joe Biden has lost delegates before the primary. In response to this many States decide to reschedule for June 2nd and June 7th. The DNC does not want primaries delayed but New York State is rich in delegates and looks again at changing the primary date. The DNC argues that rather than delay effective measures to protect public health should be put in place as was the case in Wisconsin recently. The DNC commits to funding to support States in the changes in voting formats. If 25 percent of States declare an emergency, and all States currently have, then a bill written to this effect would effectively become law. It could be looked at today, April 20th, when the Senate ends the current recess.

In all of this we must remember that until a vaccine or effective treatment is found, the USA, like other countries, must practise "social-distancing, shielding and self-isolation." This is thought to be around 12 months away and vaccinating the world's population is a massive task and will take years perhaps. New York expects the virus to peak around April 28th – the original primary date!

New York on March 30th has nearly 60,000 cases sick in hospitals and/or on ventilators. Unable to vote for anyone.

With the race for nomination decided it still is important for Biden and Sanders to gather delegates. Stripping States of delegates if they vote after June 9th would take at least 191 delegates out, and if further punishment for campaigning in later voting States took out even more the effect overall would be damaging. New York, Kentucky, and Louisiana have 382 delegates on offer which is more than Texas and close to California's. Of further consideration is the possibility that Joe Biden or Bernie Sanders could contract Coronavirus. Prime Minister of the UK, Boris Johnson, did and spent several days in intensive care where it could have gone either way. Of course, he recovered but recovery is a lengthy process even though he returned to work in an earlier course than he maybe should have.

As of 26th April 2020, current standings are:

2,415 delegates declared.

1,991 required a win.

Joe Biden has 1,305.

The competition for the nomination is over as we know but Biden must still acquire 1,991 delegates. Bernie Sanders (and others) remains on the ballot to potentially gather delegates and have a voice within the party. The following primaries are upcoming and are mail vote;

April 28th – Ohio, 136 delegates.

May 2nd – Kansas, 39 delegates.

May 12th – Nebraska, 29 delegates.

According to Fox News the so-called battleground states (Wisconsin, Pennsylvania, Michigan) which put President Trump in the White House point towards him losing ground here and in national polls. Currently looks like an eight-point lead for Biden over Trump and the President's continuing handling of the virus pandemic is a key issue. A Quinnipiac poll suggests a point lead for Biden in Florida. Nationally, a mid-April NBC/Wall Street journal survey found Biden leading Trump by 49 to 42 percent. But the democratic view on Coronavirus is missing large parts of American people's views and Trump's campaign may have already begun simply in the profile of his handling of the virus. From a survey of registered voters;

26 percent trust Biden over Trump. 29 percent don't.

36 percent trust Trump over Biden. 52 percent don't.

CHAPTER 9

Airtime – April

By the last week of April, President Trump is holding two-hour daily briefings while in the overwhelming, fast-moving pandemic Joe Biden is struggling for meaningful airtime. Trump is not always successful in his briefings and notably once suggested that perhaps "a cleansing or injecting bleach" could deal with the virus. He later back tracked and said his words were taken out of context or misconstrued. Either way it was a bizarre moment. He has also refused to take questions and walked out on occasion.

CHAPTER 10

Where Things Stand

A trend coming through the surveys points at Trump being stranded in the low 40s against Biden. This is the case throughout most of his Presidency. While fully occupied with Covid-19 he appears to just keep looking to cast Joe Biden in a bad light. No focus on improving his own standings. Meanwhile Joe Biden's lack of visibility draws criticism that he coasts along on his name and former reputation as Vice-President to Obama. Some say he should sharpen up and lose the "sleepy Joe" tag. His last in-person event pre-lockdown was March 9th, 2020 and then nothing until April 15th when he held a virtual meeting with Covid-19 workers and on April 27th, Earth Day, where both were hosted from his home in Delaware. There is a circling view that in 2016 Trump got votes from some who simply disliked Clinton. This could happen of course in 2020.

A view among many is that Trump will poll around 40 percent and the final outcome will depend on the ten or so states with tight margins.[5] Trump has already lost in some swing States which he previously won from Obama.

My own view is that as the pandemic continues to rip through southern African American States, President Trump must grasp control of the situation as his success or otherwise depends on it.

The US (the President) talks opening up, but the situation is still

---

[5]NBC News and political writers/team.

bad. At the same time in late April, the UK's full lockdown is in force as they just begin to talk about the exit strategy in Scotland while the UK government holds back on any announcements until things improve. The UK government will review lockdown on 7th May. In some American States people are protesting and demanding lockdown measures are lifted which are being met with resistance as the President gives out mixed messages it seems.

Current death toll in the US is now over 50,000. In the UK statistics show that the majority of deaths are in the Black, Asian, male, and ethnic minority group. Hardest hit are also the elderly and those vulnerable with underlying health conditions.

I think many of those groups are in key battleground states and it is expected this will impact the election result come November in my view.

CHAPTER 11

A Moving Tapestry – April into May

April 29th brought with it the announcement that New York State had cancelled the Presidential Election Democratic party vote. They passed a law which removed Sanders from the ballot as he has suspended his campaign. Therefore, with only Biden on the paper there can be no vote. The State Board of Elections cancelled the election saying that it was "a beauty contest" and not affordable in the midst of the Coronavirus crisis. Sanders was furious as he missed out potentially on delegates. He voiced his view and was advised that an election with no purpose was a risk not worth taking.

The Primary will go ahead for other races but in about 20 counties where no other votes are being held they have no need to vote at all. It seems no choice for President will appear on the remaining 62 counties' papers. New York is the first State to cancel the primary while 16 have so far postponed. While postal and absentee voting is being organised, polling places in around 42 counties are to stay open for down-ballot voting. Holding down-ballot voting now for Representatives and Congress will result in lower voter numbers. State Senate, Assembly, and other votes will go ahead. Sanders argued that the new law should not apply as it is too new. It was passed on April 3rd and Sanders suspended on April 8th. At the moment Connecticut is pushing to cancel but has rescheduled the primary for August 11th. A spokesperson for the DNC David Bergstein said he will review what it means for the convention once New York State submits an updated delegate selection plan.[6]

After April 28th, when Joe Biden wins in Ohio, the current delegate count for Joe Biden is 1,420.

Bernie Sanders was on the ballot and gained 16.6 percent of the vote and four delegates while Biden's 72.4 percent of the vote gained him 96 delegates and closer to hitting the 1,991 required for the nomination.

---

[6] (Content extracted from New York Times reporting by Sydney Ember, and Thomas Kaplan contributing. Stephanie Saul who covers National Politics for the Times since 2005. Nick Corasaniti covering National Politics since 2011 and a lead reporter in 2016 covering Trump's campaign.)

CHAPTER 12

The Making of a Vice-President

Introducing the Daily Brief

With the growing impact of Coronavirus on all of our lives, the news from around the world is fast moving and ever changing. I am finding it increasingly difficult to focus on the Democratic primaries alone when so much is happening across 187 different countries! I will highlight a selection of the daily news going forward. It is very alarming to watch these events unfolding as Governments try to grasp control and protect lives. I find the whole situation very worrying while not really understanding how this can even happen in our modern world. In highlighting the daily news, I have decided to sign up for email briefings daily directly from The New York Times *on Coronavirus and Politics. So almost all the daily briefs I set out, but not limited to, is drawn from the* On Politics and Daily Brief Teams *and I really admire the style of reporting in detailed facts. I have no political leaning either way in the US and merely try to follow what is unfolding. I am going to split the daily brief into two sections of the United States and The Rest of the World. More and more reading to do each morning.*

DB April 30th, 2020

- A tentative trial on a drug used in the past as a HIV, Ebola treatment is being trialled for treating Covid-19. Remdesivir has shown in early trials it may help.
- In France, the centralised state government is questioning why PPE (personal protective equipment) ran short. The death toll is currently 23,600.
- On Wall Street, US data showed the economy shrank by 4.8 percent in the first quarter of the year. Worst drop since 2008.
- Meanwhile, for Joe Biden pressure grows to address an allegation of sexual assault made by Tara Reade, a former aide in his Senate office, but he remains silent.

Choosing a Vice President – The Vetting Team

April 30th, 2020, Joe Biden names four people who will head up a team to start searching for and vetting possible Vice President's to be his running mate. Former Connecticut Senator Chris Dodd, Delaware representative Lisa Blunt Rochester, Los Angeles Mayor Eric Garcetti, and Apple executive and former aide to Joe Biden, Cynthia Hogan. Cynthia Hogan will serve as co-chair of the committee. They will work with vetting teams led by former White House counsel Dana Remus and former Homeland security advisor Lisa Monaco. They will collect and evaluate information on each of Joe Biden's options for candidacy to help him make his informed decision. Campaign manager Jen O'Malley Dillon and Joe Biden are fully aware of the importance of this decision in a Presidential election. To note perhaps that Joe Biden has pledged to choose a woman and the diversity and strength of his four co-chairs on the committee reflect this. He is perhaps going to name his running mate before the convention in August and make it known he is looking for someone supportive of where he wants to take the country forward. In all likelihood he could name 12 to 15 options but realistically will look seriously at 6 to 11 candidates. He could look at Senate or State Governors and early names in the picture are;

Senators Kamala Harris, California, Elizabeth Warren, Massachusetts. Governor of Michigan Gretchen Whitmer, and Stacy Adams, formerly a candidate for Governor.[7]

Elizabeth Warren has indicated her interest and would accept if asked. An African American and female running mate is suggested and Lisa Blunt Rochester of the vetting team fits this profile.

Alongside the former announcement Joe Biden is facing mounting pressure to address an allegation of sexual assault from Tara Reade. Her claim dates back to 1993 when she was working for Joe Biden. He stays silent, however. Progressive activists and women's rights are debating how best to handle this allegation while mindful that President Trump faced multiple allegations through his Presidency and Joe Biden has just one. He has previously been praised by women's groups as being an outspoken champion for survivors of sexual violence but with two women corroborating Tara Reade's story Joe Biden stays silent. The feeling among aides is that it is not significant regarding votes and the private view is that he has said "it did not happen." Tara Reade worked for Joe Biden in the Senate office in the early nineties and brought her allegation in March 2020.[8]

---

[7] Extract Matt Rourke/PA and Steven Senne/AP.
[8] Max Whittaker, NYT.

Onwards – Tara Reade and Joe Biden

DB May 1st 2020

- Whitehouse and Republican Governors are angling towards cautious reopening of the economy while G.O.P. Leaders in Congress have tried to slow future federal stimulus spending as the polls suggest otherwise.
- An additional 3.8 million file for unemployment, yet the S & P 500 closed on April 30th with the best monthly rise since 1987 of 13%. Suggests confidence from investors that business will return sooner than thought.
- As National stay-at-home guidelines expire, more than 20 States keep them in force.
- The US or President Trump escalates his blame campaign on China causing the virus. Studies so far point at live animal markets in Wuhan.
- Europe is reporting the worst economic downturn which could see the eurozone shrink by 12%. In the world half a billion more people could be pushed into poverty.
- India reports biggest single day rise in cases.
- London bus drivers demand more PPE.

DB May 2nd 2020

- Fox News Axelrod said the Reade claim never came up in the vetting process of Joe Biden in 2008 and Joe Biden asks the secretary of Senate to locate papers relevant to any claim.
- Remdesivir. In the US drug trials backed by federal money are testing an old drug used for HIV and Ebola in the fight against

Covid-19. Will not be a vaccine but hopes for a cure or treatment.
- ❏ President Trump takes hard action on China. Malaysia rounds up immigrants, Singapore plans to ease restrictions soon. In the UK Prime Minister Boris Johnson sets out a roadmap to exit lockdown in three stages only when the R rate (rate it is passed from person to person) is below 1.

DB May 4th 2020

- ❏ After Wall Street reports the best April for decades, the futures market takes a dip and economies around the world shrink.
- ❏ Italy begins to reopen in chaos. Takeout food only and hygiene restrictions are difficult to control, especially for small businesses to fund as well.

Tara Reade Allegations

By 1st May 2020, while Donald Trump flounders in the public's falling confidence, he has lashed out at aides and lost out to Joe Biden in key State primaries, while the jobless numbers continue to grow, the public are afraid and looking for better leadership and government. Joe Biden's biggest challenge at the moment seems to be the Tara Reade allegations which will not go away, and he breaks his silence simply saying, "this never happened." A statement was reported in Medium. Biden calls on the National Archives to release any existing information on the existing complaint related to the allegation. In recent days Biden has appeared in virtual fundraisers and on TV. When asked to make papers available from his Senate papers he said that personal details would not be in there and therefore called on The National Archives. Tara Reade keeps changing her story. A few people have corroborated her story though. Mr Biden acknowledges that women who make allegations should be heard, not silenced. But he raises doubt and questions the growing contradictions of her account of events. Speaker Nancy Pelosi is keen to let voices of women be heard, has the highest regard for Joe Biden, and reiterates her respect for the "me too" campaign while staying fair to Joe Biden. Curiously, Trump says Biden should address it face on and "it could be false."[9]

---

[9] Katie Glueck, NYT.

CHAPTER 13

Patchwork Reopening?

On the 1st May more than half of States move to reopen business and protestors, some armed, entered Michigan's State Capital to oppose stay-at-home orders. Texas allows nearly all businesses to open this morning, with a few restrictions, while in swathes of upstate communities hardly touched by the virus are more worried about the economy than lives. An upstate backlash grows in New York over the shutdown. The quest for a cure or vaccine sees laboratories across the US join the federal initiative to study Coronavirus genome. Looking to trace patterns of transmission, investigate outbreaks, and mapping out how the virus is evolving could help find the elusive cure.

In some States, shops, hairdressers, and beauty parlours are opening and people must decide whether to return to work as money is much needed or stay home to stay safe. Texas and Ohio have joined the growing list of States where restaurants, theatres, and malls are opening at 25 percent capacity in a few days. Georgia allows full restarts for all businesses. Currently 50/50 on opening or staying in lockdown across the country.

Also, today (2nd May) it is reported that Tara Reade allegedly told her brother and some friends at the time of Joe Biden's sexual assault. They confirm her story and Joe Biden continues his denial that it happened. Collin Moulton spoke to the Washington Post about the matter and suggests that as Joe Biden is running for the highest office then the allegations need to be fully and transparently investigated and with full cooperation from the

Democratic Party. Miss Reade's story, dating from 1993, keeps changing, there is no proof to date and as the complaint was only made in March 2020 it is unlikely any court will rule against Biden.[10]

Joe Biden served 36 years in the Senate, any records that exist will be in the National Archives. 2,000 boxes and more than 400 gigabytes of data were turned over to Delaware University and as it is not catalogued it is a huge task to search for evidence far less proof. Trump has been habitually cleared of several such allegations and even he considered this one could be false. In 2016, before Joe Biden was considered as Vice President to Obama, he was thoroughly vetted and none of the allegations came up then! Joe Biden is thought to resist scrutiny of historic Senate papers as he feels the content could potentially be used against him by Trump. Even with assurances that only papers relating to Tara Reade would be searched, everyone accepts that leaks happen.

Primaries update: In Kansas, Biden wins 29 delegates and now holds 1,435

Bernie Sanders and Elizabeth Warren remained on the ballot with Hawaii representative Tulsi Gabbard. The vote was entirely by mail and as such a high turnout compared to 2016. Fox News reports that Elizabeth Warren denounces Tara Reade's allegations as nonsense and supports Joe Biden. Elizabeth Warren is thought to be on the short list for Vice President (running mate), but it is unlikely to be announced who he will pick until July. Other supporters include Hillary Clinton and Senator Amy Klobuchar while Biden makes it known he supports women's rights movements, including the "me too" movement.[11]

---

[10] New York Times.
[11] Vandana Rambaran.

DB 4th to 7th May 2020

- Around the world social distancing and hygiene requirements are making it very difficult for many small businesses.
- In the UK, as Prime Minister Boris Johnson speaks of his ordeal and real fear of dying from Covid-19, he thanks the medical staff who saved him. He names his new-born son after two Doctors in particular, both called Nick. The baby's full name is Wilfred Laurie Nicholas.
- London bus drivers are fearful after it is announced that 29 London bus drivers have so far died from Covid-19.
- Germany, Italy, Greece, and Spain begin to reopen and children in Germany can return to school in small numbers.
- In Spain, small stores and hair salons can reopen. In Italy people can visit relatives in their own area.
- Australia and New Zealand look to allow air travel between their countries. France reports a test showing a case of Coronavirus in a patient in December 2019.
- In America, George W Bush called on all Americans to rally behind the government and fight the virus together. The Trump administration predicts the death toll from the virus could reach 3,000 daily deaths by early June yet continues to urge reopening. Markets predict positive signs for Wall Street and European markets. Airlines burn through ten billion dollars a month; stocks gain but Disney's profit plunges 91 per cent.

DB 8th to 18th May 2020

- Reports emerge of a form of the virus which children can transmit, and many are in hospital in New York with illness linked to Covid-19.

- The UK and National governments look at how to ease lockdown. Scotland's First Minister Nicola Sturgeon rules out easing for Scotland as it is too soon.
- Angela Merkel in Germany announces the return of the Bundesliga this month.
- In the US Trump announces he is winding down the Coronavirus taskforce. He is likely leaving the issue with state governors and eyeing up his re-election campaign. Meanwhile, figures show the US unemployment rate hit 14.7 percent and 20.5 million jobs lost in April. Job losses across hospitality, manufacturing, retails, industries, and white-collar workers in business sectors. The unemployment rate for blacks is 16.7 percent, for Hispanic or Latino it is 18.9 percent. On Wall Street stocks tumble as the Federal Reserve warns lawmakers must protect the economy. House Democrats announce a three trillion-dollar relief fund, which House Republicans declare exorbitant. Trump signs a two trillion-dollar economic rescue package.
- Retail sales plunge and Wall Street is poised for a drop. However, FTSE, DAX and Nikkei all closed on a small rise.
- Germany is entering recession and China's economy shows signs of recovery. Japan enters recession.
- In the Primaries in the US Biden continues to secure delegates and is urged to be more proactive and begin a campaign. Trump is focusing on the economy and Covid-19 and is also urged to up his game.

DB 18th May to 31st May 2020

- Britain's economy is expected to contract by 30%, being the worst result since 1706.

- The infection rate in Germany has been rising after lockdown was eased a little.
- China offers to help North Korea fight the virus.
- In the UK, the National Office for statistics finds that black people in the UK are twice as likely to die from Covid-19 than white people. The UK health service investigates tracking app for Smartphone users.
- Meanwhile President Trump talks of "bounce back" for the economy while poverty and suffering grow in the key battleground States, ripping through the Black, African American, and minority ethnic groups (BAME.) Deaths rise in States that are opening, chaos all around the country and President Obama calls Trump out for the mayhem.
- UK Prime Minister Boris Johnson announces a change to the lockdown measures and how they will ease gradually. Travellers to Britain must have a 14-day quarantine. From 13th May some sports in England can resume with restrictions in place such as golf, tennis, and fishing but Scotland's First Minister keeps Scotland in Lockdown with the only measure being exercise outside is now unlimited and not just once per day.
- France begins to ease lockdown.
- Germany's infection rate rises slightly amid their easing measures.

Coronavirus cases worldwide now stand at four million across 177 countries and more than a quarter of a million people have died.

I find this so very sad, frightening and simply horrifying. The speed of transmission around the world is just awful. There is a sense of ... what? I don't really know but confusion, anger, panic even in some people. Most of all I am feeling fear and sadness at so much heartache.

New York City in May 2020

❏ It has been found that New York City looks like the epicentre and that the virus has spread to most other States from New York City through travel. It is unlikely to look at reopening any time soon as in other countries any easing of lockdown brings a rise in cases. Churches in Georgia remain closed. White House staff wear masks as Covid-19 positive cases are found in the White House staff and US advisors say a vaccine is unlikely to be found in time to allow students to return to education in the fall. Further, Trump's administration/advisors warn that the virus is a long way from being controlled.

❏ In late May in the UK the New York Times reported that the National Health Service is hailed as the new "Church". Years of austerity, dilapidated buildings, and overworked staff has now become the nations' focus in the fight against the virus. Many fundraisers for the NHS emerge, not least Captain Tom Moore who raises over 30 million pounds with a charity walk in his back garden. Captain Tom wanted to raise one thousand pounds before his 100th birthday.

❏ In the US, the virus is rampaging through Latin America where they don't have sufficient resources to deal with it and are suffering huge loss of life. In New York, State health officials are investigating over 100 cases of a rare but dangerous inflammatory syndrome affecting children and linked to Covid - 19. The chief medical officer, Dr Faucii, disagrees with President Trump and deems easing lockdown measures too fast and too soon which will in his view bring suffering and death as Trump says it is safe for students and children to return to school and Obama calls Trump's administration "clueless" and not very good at what they do. Doctors report a flurry of strokes in younger patients, adding to thoughts that the virus can also attack kidneys, brain, heart and liver. All this as the chairman of the US Federal Reserve expects the US

- economy to return but that the downturn could last all the way to the end of 2021.
- The war of words between China and President Trump continues as he blames them and calls for an inquiry into the origins and spread of Coronavirus.
- Around the world in late May Germany's infection rate triples in 24 hours as they ease lockdown further.
- Scotland is still in strict lockdown and trying to drive down the "R" rate (rate which one person infects others) In London now fewer than 24 cases of Covid-19 reported per day when at the peak it was around 230,000. London is hopeful of being virus free by June.
- There are new clusters of the virus in China and Brazil struggles with a rising death rate to now 2nd worst in the world, only passed by the US. Hotspots also emerge in Africa.
- In France children returning to school bring 70 positive tests for Coronavirus and lockdown is brought back in.
- The WHO agrees to begin an inquiry into the global pandemic and response to it and in particular, China.
- Germany puts Europe first and backs a 500 billion Euro recovery fund where a transfer of funds from rich to poorer countries and borrowing from the EU as a collective proves not popular in Germany.
- Researchers worldwide continue the quest for a vaccine and some positive hopes arise. Track and trace processes are put in place in Paris after strict lockdown eases and cases fall.
- President Trump continues his rhetoric and unhappiness with China and WHO, threatening to pull funds permanently, accusing them of bias and a burning dependency on China. Federal Reserves in the US are worried about the economy, bankruptcy, and long-term unemployment as are many countries. Treasury secretary Steven Munchin warns of

permanent damage to the US economy. The search for a vaccine finds hope from researchers at Harvard University who have successfully tested a vaccine on monkeys, and it protected them from infection of Covid-19.

- By the last week of May, President Trump is banning travel into the US from Brazil as cases spike. Americans, with most States now open, look to celebrate Memorial Day weekend as the country reaches 100,000 deaths due to Coronavirus. 700,000 new cases around the world in the last week.
- But in France, Italy, Spain, and the UK, cases are falling as lockdown slowly eases.
- A row in London over Boris Johnson's key advisor erupts as he admits breaking lockdown rules. He states his case over why but refuses to apologise or resign.
- Japan lifts the state of emergency, easing restrictions and restarts domestic flights with temperature checks at airports.

CHAPTER 14

The Vice President and Michelle Obama

Now in the first week of May on the campaign trail, Joe Biden is working with his committee and looking into any interest Michelle Obama has in the position as running mate/Vice President. While he thinks it unlikely the committee are keen to garner any media attention they can for candidates likely to have the power to help Biden defeat Trump. Michelle Obama is a trusted and known leader with strength to deal with the lies and rhetoric emanating from the White House. She would be an asset for the Democratic party throughout all States and while Joe Biden would choose her in a moment and not just because she ticks all his boxes as being female and black African/American. She is trusted, respected, but so far not making any noises about wanting to revisit The White House. The committee would like at this point to have more input and support from both the Obamas and try to reignite a buzz among voters. Joe Biden still has a dozen or so candidates in mind but will probably not choose or declare his choice until around sometime in July. It may be that Michelle and Barack Obama know this and are also waiting a bit longer before throwing support in or expressing interests.

Early May Reopening

During the first week of May many States continue pushing ahead with reopening, in spite of the growing number of cases and deaths which some people agree with, some do not. At the same time other countries are reporting big spikes in cases with India seeing its biggest single day jump and Russia reporting cases now over 10,000. Britain has a rising death toll and catching up to the tragic death toll of Italy even though the UK has a younger population. The virus death rate among the over 70s is particularly high and in Britain the over 70s and vulnerable have been advised to shield/isolate totally for many months and yet the figures are appalling. In America, this week tens of thousands of new cases are reported with 1,400 deaths reported from Coronavirus on 2nd May alone. Yet still President Trump pushes on with reopening to try and save the economy and bring America back from the worst slump since the 1930s. What is the cost to human life?

Is it possible perhaps that while the UK Prime Minister Boris Johnson looks to set out his roadmap out of lockdown on 7th May, President Trump is trying to show he can do it better? Perhaps, but each country should follow their own needs, in my opinion! Congress has now weighed in on the divide between States who want to reopen and those that don't. The Republican-majority Senate will reopen on Monday May 11th while the Democratic-controlled House of Representatives will stay closed. The Senate decision to reconvene with just 100 Senators portrays the image that America is back in business, which is what Trump wants.

Figures around the world stand at 3.5 million infections, with 247,000 deaths reported by governments including 67,000 in the US. [12]

Again, in my opinion, it is hard to understand the President's wish to forge ahead with opening in such desperate times. Perhaps he is doing the Democrats a favour as his popularity seems to be falling with any real campaign by the Democrats at all.

Just at the end of the first week in May, Texas' stay-at-home orders expired just one day after the state reported their highest

---

[12] Associated press journalists around the world.

death toll and cases jumped up by 1,033 to a new high after three weeks when stay-at-home orders were in place. Governor Abbot orders reopening. Retail, movie venues, malls, museums, and libraries to reopen to 25 per cent capacity. Churches and places of worship to remain open. Across the State some comply, and some cities stay "closed." It is reported from the UK that United Airlines will not fly from New York, Newark to Edinburgh, Scotland until at least October. It is worth noting that in very general terms Republican-ruled States are more likely to reopen than otherwise. The only caveat to Republican Texas governor Grey Abott's strategy is that he is cautiously reopening. Counties with less than five active cases can go to 50 per cent capacity, which now applies to nearly half of Texas' 254 counties and 30 million population. Beaches, hair salons, bars and restaurants remain closed. The next phase is due around May 18th and in Texas today, 5th May, figures reported are: 27,000 cases and 750 deaths. [13]

Winding Down the Coronavirus Taskforce and Implications

President Trump indicates he is winding down the Coronavirus task force. Medical advisors, however, predict a huge surge in cases is coming. Students will be unlikely to return to colleges in the fall. Student loan debts will rise hugely, and college budgets are likely to be slashed. The so-called public higher education could well be out of reach for most of the country. Joe Biden has made college education costs a key part of his campaign and future focus for America. This stance from Trump could see him lose more popularity perhaps. Currently it looks like the polls say 42 percent of Americans are happy with Trump's handling of the

---

[13] ABC News: Stengle from Dallas, Weber from Austin.

crisis, but this is down nine points from March. Democrats are more likely to say the federal government's efforts are not enough while Republicans are likely to say it is enough.

CHAPTER 15

Campaigning Virtually

With the usual form of campaigning and fundraisers closed down due to the fear and confinements of the pandemic, Joe Biden is forced to follow many around the world and work virtually. On 5th May a campaign fundraiser with Joe Biden and special guest Senator Amy Klobuchar offered the Zoom link to supporters for a co-host contribution of $20,000, Champion $5,600, Sponsor $2,800, and an Advocate $1,000. The invites were sent out two weeks in advance. Amy Klobuchar is from Minnesota and in the frame as a potential running mate for Joe Biden. These events are usually of course hosted somewhere grand, full of razmataz, and carrying huge costs. So, the move onto Zooms with a minimum contribution from attendees of $1,000 and hosted from his own home is a very lucrative event. This one is thought to have raised $1.5 million! Zoom is a huge boost to his ability to reach $1,000 contributors. Joe Biden has hosted around 20 such Zoom fundraisers and his wife Jill has also attended about 12 of them. On occasions there is a "meet and greet" prior to the main event. Campaign manager Jennifer O'Malley has a growing list of contacts who wish to attend future events on Zoom. Some notable attendees are the aforementioned Klobuchar, former rival Pete Buttigeig, and President Obama. He also has some celebrity input with a recent event kicking off with an introduction by actor Billy Porter, a performance by Melissa Etheridge and Kristen Chenoweth, and an appearance by Billie Jean King who was standing in front of her wall of trophies. That event is thought to have drawn in $1.1 million. [14]

Meanwhile, as the virus continues to grow and wreak havoc, causing death, hardship, and cases of social and racial injustices in the States and around the world, President Trump determines that getting the economy moving is a must. He and Vice President Mike Pence began to travel around the country with Trump visiting a mask-making plant in Arizona and chose not to wear a mask himself while the Vice President visited medical facilities and manufacturing plants in Minnesota, Wisconsin, and Indiana. He has further plans to meet with Faith leaders next week in Iowa. The mid-Western States will of course be crucial in the election campaign. Also, having announced he was closing down the Covid-19 taskforce, President Trump reverses his decision as he is urged by many, including medical people, to keep it going. Trump is looking to promote tax cuts in his campaign while Democratic legislatures are looking for direct funding of benefits to help those affected by the pandemic and for an increase in food stamps to see people through the economic crisis. Nationwide now Joe Biden's lead over Trump seems to be growing according to a Monmouth University Poll. But interestingly the views on the Tara Reade situation reads that 37 per cent said it's maybe true, 32 per cent said probably not true, and 31 per cent had no opinion either way. Trump's standing among women appears weaker than Biden's.

Other negative press for Trump surrounds Republican Senator Kelly Loeffler of Georgia, a former business executive and perhaps the richest member of the Senate, finds that her finances are under scrutiny and dragging down her approval numbers just a month before she faces her voters. Both her and her husband traded millions of dollars of stock right as the Coronavirus briefings began and were forced to deny allegations of insider trading. When Loeffler left her business for public office in the Senate she was gifted $9 million by her employer. The company is

---

[14] New York Times; Giovanni Russonello.

run by her husband, but she claimed financial sacrifice in order to serve in public office. She tried to deflect attention by announcing she used her private plane to bring home stranded Georgians to the US after the virus situation left them stranded around the world and donated her Senate salary to Covid-19 causes, while making further charitable donations of $1 million to other causes.[15]

Moving Through May and Campaigning in a Pandemic

Today in the UK BBC News reports that President Obama announces strong criticism for President Trump's handling of the virus, calling it a "chaotic disaster" as CNN reports he said that in a call while asking his former staff to work for Joe Biden. Predictably, The White House hits back swiftly, saying Trump's unprecedented actions have saved lives.

The US now has 77,000 deaths and 1.2 million confirmed cases with some States opening and cases continuing to rise.

Obama goes on to accuse Trump of a "what's in it for me" attitude which draws a further response of saying Obama's handling of the Swine Flu in days past was "disastrous." All this does nothing to help Trump's continuing and falling popularity which has gone from 49 percent in March to around 43 percent today. Swing States show a shift towards Biden, sparking fury among the Trump campaign, especially the campaign manager Brad Pascale. Republican Senator David Perdue floated that Georgia could be in play which has been a traditionally red state, but Trump only beat Hillary Clinton by five points in 2016. Not good news for the increasingly faltering President but encouraging for the Democrats. Where Trump led in Florida in March he now trails Biden. Trump officials dismiss it and say things will look very

---

[15] New York Times; Nicholas Fandos, Congressional Correspondent.

different in November. Throughout his term in office Trump has been basking in a strong economy but, regardless, the election and his re-election seems to hang on the outcome and handling of the Pandemic. While he tries to keep blaming the Chinese for the trouble of the virus, the fact is the US has lost around 26.5 million jobs in five weeks. As cases jump amid openings in Florida, with 802 new cases and 46 deaths in just three days, the virus has reached The White House. A White House staffer tested positive after contact with health official Anthony Fauci. In addition, an aide of the President's tested positive after contact he had contact with him, prompting the President to have a test himself which came back negative.

CHAPTER 16

Mail-in Voting in all Primaries – May

By mid-May, with White House staffers testing positive for Coronavirus, the focus is turning among all parties to mail-in voting as in-person voting causes fear, alarm, and distress across the country. This presents a whole new bag of problems just as the President looks to try and up his game after stinging criticism from not just President Obama but from many across parties. In Wisconsin, the mail-in ballot brought a higher-than-normal turnout than usual, and the Trump camp is all too aware that in swing States this will perhaps help the Democrats' cause but not his own. Dr Anthony Fauci voices his views that opening up is premature, and the risk of more needless suffering and death must be considered. The virus has spread most quickly in densely populated areas and is particularly cruel to black and other ethnic minorities who are already those at risk in poorer areas with underlying health issues, low income, and poor healthcare which also tend to be the traditionally blue or "swing States." Trump bellowing that the Republican states are in good order does nothing but further alienate a lot of voters.

In the Nebraska primary Joe Biden wins, gaining 29 delegates, with 76.1% of the vote, Sanders 14% of the vote, and Warren 6.3% of the vote.

On the running mate question, Kamala Harris, having initially been discounted due to a previous run-in with Joe Biden, appears to have re-entered the bid and looks like a top pick at the moment. Harris ticks the boxes which Joe Biden set out previously, being the daughter of immigrant parents from India and Jamaica. At aged 55, with a President in his 70s, it is thought to be a good balance by many.[16]

The Oregon Primary result sees Biden take 43 delegates with none for Sanders, Warren, or Tulsi Gabbard.

Joe Biden now has 1,507 of the required 1,991 delegates. With 2,662 so far declared, the split is Sanders 984, Warren 81, Bloomberg 55, Buttigieg 26 and Klobuchar 7.

Joe Biden is enjoying some support from a former hopeful, Pete Buttigieg. While he pulled out of the race he is committed to running fundraisers and campaigning events for Biden, seeing his role in the party as "being useful." Further, he is throwing his weight into a 'Win the Era' initiative which seeks to treat the Presidency as not just the only office that matters but will be formed with Supervisors in County Offices which will help support at more local levels, especially through the pandemic. Some areas of concern or need could be delivering a vaccine and running a contact trace and test system. Further issues on the minds of both Presidential candidates could and definitely should be Debt Relief. How and what is the way forward for the country? While the US continues to engage in the spat with China over the virus, some fear the US is coming across in a bad light. President Trump should maybe be trying to take a more prominent role as a world leader and restore some confidence, not just at home but globally, that the US President and leader of the free world is competent and trustworthy. Pete Buttigieg is also behind the drive to change old outdated systems in the Electoral College and a case is currently being heard in the Supreme Court (late May 2020.)

Political views turn again to the subject of who will be Vice President with the same names in the frame. Elizabeth Warren, Massachusetts, Kamala Harris, California, and Stacy Abrams,

---

[16] New York Times; Christopher Cadelago, Natasha Korecki. Politico.

former governor of Georgia. There is an excitement among the party and voters that if he does indeed choose one of those who are all thought to be a bit more progressive then that can only help his cause in the race to The White House. "Move On" members also suggest Michelle Obama (again), Bernie Sanders, Susan Rice, and Katie Porter.

Over the last 10 days of May President Trump voices again his opposition and reluctance to postal voting not least because he knows it will hurt him and threatens to withhold federal funding to support it. He did, however, later backtrack from that particular threat. More people are voting postally than in person in the current range of primaries.[17]

While the CDC releases guidelines for reopening public accommodation and business over the coming weekend, Trump denounces them, saying it could slow recovery and cross into religious liberty. *The plan is in three phases and looks sensible in my opinion.* It is all at the State governor's discretion. Trump also confirms that the Republican Party Convention will go ahead on the planned date in August but will, in deference to the pandemic, be a scaled down event. As support for Trump falls further, he accuses Fox News of not doing anything to support him or assist in him winning the election. If Biden was to win the Presidency, Senate would be the only backstop between Democratic full control of the executive and legislative branches. Trump has moved the Republican coalition toward male and less educated voters while the party's advantage among older voters is disappearing. As Trump's popularity drops so too does support for Republican Governors.

---

[17] New York Times; Reid J. Epstein, Nick Corasaniti, Annie Karnie.

Hawaii Primary Result May 24th 2020

Joe Biden 16 delegates, Bernie Sanders eight delegates.

Current position with 1,075 still at stake;

Biden 1,489, Sanders 984, Warren 55, Buttigeig 26.

In order to secure the required 1,991 delegates Joe Biden must secure around 50 percent of the remaining delegates otherwise pledged and super delegates, of which there are 771, Democratic lawmakers and party members will cast their votes at the Convention in July bringing the total number of delegates to 4,750. This would mean the candidate would need 2,375 in order to win.

It may not come to that.

CHAPTER 17

As May Ends, Where Are We Now?

The Coronavirus has completely taken over governments around the world, changed the economy and jobs, and brought to attention some social and racial injustices to name but a few issues. Healthcare and the great divide between the rich and the poor are becoming ever more relevant. In the US in election year, it is unprecedented and damaging in ways that perhaps only history can recount. *Both campaigns are evolving through the pandemic and are more reactive than proactive in my view, with the handling of the virus and the economy the key factors.* However, it is reported that among voters only 50 percent said it is a key issue although 72 percent recognise it as a factor. Both Democrats and Republicans seem to think that so far the President's performance and handling of the crisis is terrible, which would explain his falling ratings. The general view appears to be that Trump needs to find renewed support from the swing States, from the media, and indeed from some Republicans. Joe Biden also must secure support in the swing States and find a strong running mate. Either way, Trump must do all of it while gaining control of the virus and restart the ailing economy. As lockdowns ease and some hope of recovery dawns, perhaps ratings will recover. But many swing States run by Democratic governors are devastated by the virus. Ratings have surged in Wisconsin, Michigan, and Pennsylvania but in Georgia and Florida the opposite is happening where Republican governors flouting social distancing measures in favour of opening up are seeing better ratings.[18]

DB 1st to 7th June 2020

❏   In the first week of May in the US, amid all of the virus chaos, a white police officer was filmed arresting a black man (who was suspected of passing a fake $20 bill) and was kneeling on his neck. George Floyd died, and the arresting officer was charged.

❏   Riots raged for the whole week not just in the US, but anger grows as Berlin, London, and Vancouver also decry the killing.

❏   China and Iran accuse the US of hypocrisy on human rights. Violent demonstrations and looting continue.

❏   President Trump decides to arrange a press call or a stunt, whichever you want to call it, and has the security and military clear him a path to take a short walk from the White House to pose outside a Church holding a bible. This could become a defining image of his demise, who knows! Trump is condemned for not responding appropriately. This dominates the news from the US for the week. In fact, he threatens to call in the military to deal with what he calls a group of "fascists." By 5th June, demonstrators pour into the streets across the US in a tenth night of protests at the killing of George Floyd in late May. This is the dominating story. Democrats in Congress plan to unveil legislation addressing police brutality. Trust between communities and police is fast disappearing.

❏   Around the world outrage grows at the situation in America.

❏   The European Union is planning a ground-breaking recovery plan involving all 27 member states. 750 billion Euros in the first initiative where funds are raised for a common debt.

---

[18] New York Times. Author.

- Japan approves a $296 billion supplementary budget to help fund $1.1 trillion in recovery measures.
- In the UK, the Dominic Cummings story of the Prime Minister's senior advisor breaking lockdown rules continues to cause trouble for Boris Johnson.
- Moscow reopens parks, shopping malls, car dealerships, and other businesses. Moscow accounts for almost half of the country's reported Coronavirus cases which is offered as 414,878 cases. Putin is at his lowest approval rating yet and sets a July 1st date for a referendum which could keep him in power until 2036.

DB 8th to 16th June 2020

- It is announced that the US economy entered recession in February 2020. The pandemic could shrink the economy globally by 5.2 percent this year. Demonstrations over the killing of George Floyd continue as lawmakers prepare legislation to make it easier to prosecute police officers found to have violated civil rights. It is proposed that one measure could be to ban "chokeholds." Nine members of the Minneapolis City Council pledge to dismantle the police department and replace them with a new system of ensuring public safety.
- Angela Merkel declined an invitation to attend a group seven meeting in Washington DC, citing Covid-19 issues but news that around 9,500 US troops will leave the country points at floundering trust in the trans-Atlantic alliance. Also considered a response to the President's threat to pull US funding from the World Health Organisation. And, after three months of hardship, New York, the centre of the world's largest outbreak, starts to ease lockdown with workers returning to manufacturing, retail, and construction.

- Wall Street and Asian stocks Inch higher on Monday 8th while European markets were mostly down.
- New Zealand declares the country is Covid free. In a population of five million, recording just 22 deaths is truly amazing and a testimony to the strict lockdown imposed very early in the outbreak in the country. Prime Minister Jacinda Ardern is not complacent and the work to keep the country virus free will continue.
- Around the world many see Trump's threat to pull funding from the WHO as confirmation of his mistakes catching up with him and looking to blame others. Americans feel that the country is let down by the beleaguered President.
- Angela Merkel's actions set out above are causing him further harm.
- Beijing seized on the moment to portray what it sees as America's hypocrisy and decline while promoting their own authoritarian system and therefore ignoring their own problems with China who have imposed new security laws on Hong Kong.
- In Britain, Parliament returns with strict social distancing measures in place causing havoc when MP's must vote. Huge lines form.
- Paris opens cafes for outdoor seating areas and service after 11 weeks of lockdown.
- A fresh outbreak of Ebola occurs in the Congo. It is also dealing with the world's largest measles outbreak and the pandemic.

DB 17th to 24th June 2020

- Rows over racial injustices and police brutality dominates in the US. The military official, General Mark A Milley, apologised for his part in walking with President Trump to the Church so he could pose with a Bible, regretting possibly that it became politicized.

- The Black Lives Matter movement grows and hope in Joe Biden grows while Trump flounders further in the polls. He is not thought to be against police reform, but many feel he is not effective or convincing in this regard. Something has gone very wrong in America with law enforcement. After years of growth for the Trump administration he is now facing the reality that the virus, crashing economy, and racial and social injustices has brought him to a worse position than in 2016 when he vowed to make America great.

- Meanwhile Joe Biden and his supporters are committed to bringing reform and change.

- Officials across America are announcing major police reforms. Governor of New York Andrew Cuomo warns that not sticking to social distancing rules to attempt to contain the virus will slow down the city's reopening. The US food and drugs agency revoked the use of two drugs used in the treatment of Malaria in the treatment of Covid-19 as they are unlikely to be effective.

- In a milestone ruling the Supreme Court rules that Civil Rights Act of 1964 which prohibits sex discrimination applies to gay and transgender and protects from workplace discrimination which is hailed as a victory for the L.G.B.T.Q. community.

- New Coronavirus cases in the US account for 20 percent of new worldwide cases. The US accounts for 4.3 percent of the world's population so a proportionately high number of infections. President Trump signed an executive order to suspend several categories of foreign work visas until the end of 2020. It is intended to boost jobs in the US.

- In mid-May Beijing sees a surge in virus cases and lockdown returns. 79 infections all traced to Xinfadi food market which is now closed again.

- ❏ Some European borders open while the figures show eight million infections worldwide and 430,000 deaths to Covid-19. Two million cases and 170,000 deaths have been in Europe.
- ❏ European cities continue to see violent demonstrations and statues of historical figures linked to slavery and colonialism are being toppled, vandalised, and it seems like the tensions of the pandemic and racial injustices which began in America are causing many to try to rewrite history. Hardship and suffering all around.
- ❏ In the UK Brexit talks continue as Boris Johnson meets with EU leaders to discuss the approach to trade talks. Both sides seek a deal, but it is not going to be easy. July and August will see serious discussion.
- ❏ A summit between the EU and China on 22nd May proves fruitless. Having been postponed since March there is still no movement on any issues of state subsidies, technology, climate change, or equal opportunities.
- ❏ Norway, Denmark, and Finland all close their borders to Sweden as Coronavirus cases grow in Sweden who have not embraced full lockdown. They are trying to protect lives and the economy at the same time which only time will tell us if the policy works. Sweden now has twice as many infections and five times the deaths of the other three nations combined! [19]

DB 25th to 30th June 2020

- ❏ By the 29th of June, the world tally of Covid-19 cases reached 10 million.
- ❏ In Scotland, where lockdown has continued more strictly than other parts of the United Kingdom, cases are falling and no deaths for three days at the end of June. First Minister Nicola Sturgeon is

---

[19] Figures reported New York Times.

determined to follow her advisors and scientific advice and will not be pushed by the Prime Minister Boris Johnson.

- In England, the City of Leicester suffers a new outbreak just a few weeks after lockdown measures are eased and the city and surrounding area is forced back into lockdown.
- Meanwhile, in Europe, as reopening continues, cases begin to rise again. Germany saw a spike of 1,500 cases and put two counties back into lockdown.
- The World Health Organisation intends to send a team to China next week to investigate the origins of the virus. The Chinese government approved a human vaccine trial for one year after promising results.
- Once again in America, as cases and deaths keep growing, medical advisor Dr Anthony Fauci warns that reopening too soon is dangerous. President Trump is increasing the number of tests but also blaming the number of tests for the rising number of positive cases. Cases reach their highest point since April. It is particularly bad in the South and West. In Texas, the governor halted reopening as 4,300 people were hospitalised which is double the number at the beginning of June.
- India and Brazil are also seeing a huge rise in cases and while borders in Europe open up, the US is banned, as are travellers from Russia and other high-infection-rate countries. Cases in the US have risen by 65 percent and now total (29th June) 2.5 million.
- In other news reported today, a suspected plot of Russians paying a bounty to the Taliban for the death of US soldiers is uncovered. Cash has been discovered from Taliban outposts and information from captured militants and criminals points at Russian involvement.

CHAPTER 18

Campaigning, Covid, and Cybercrime

June begins with the President's attention very much focused on the killing of George Floyd and the resultant issues, with many calling for reform. He continues to condemn the threats and violence of demonstrations and demands law and order returns to the streets. His Twitter feed over this last weekend barely mentions the Coronavirus or the economy. But what does Joe Biden have to say? Typically, Democrats fare better in elections when a period of calm surrounds racial tension or social injustices but that may not be the case. It could be that the Millennials and Generation Z are changing the Democratic party. The governor of Minnesota (where the killing happened), Tim Walz, Democrat, spoke movingly of the history of pain and anguish but now the world is watching. Shortly afterwards the arresting officer Derek Chauvin was arrested and charged with third degree murder and manslaughter. Protests amplify and black leaders look to Joe Biden for a commitment to change. The topic of him choosing a female black running mate rears its head as it reported that Amy Klobuchar previously declined to prosecute multiple cases against white police officers and one case was in fact against Derek Chauvin. However, it appears that the case was dismissed after Klobuchar left the Senate. The story will have hurt her interests as a possible running mate. Amy Klobuchar is white.

In campaigning and Primary matters there are eight Primaries on 2nd June. Many of those were mail-in voting due to the continuing crisis and following those eight the standings are: Joe Biden

1,922, Sanders 1,013, Warren 58, Bloomberg 43.

So not far to go for Joe Biden to reach the 1,991 required for the nomination. Voting almost entirely by mail is bringing a larger than normal turn out of voters which President Trump knows can damage his cause. However, he continues to orchestrate his own demise and seems to be doing little by way of campaigning at all. In the wake of the killing of George Floyd he uses inflammatory rhetoric and has also used teargas to clear the demonstrators outside the White House to clear his path to the Church for his publicity stunt of posing with a Bible. By June 6th it is announced once all mail-in ballots are counted and confirmed from 2nd June that Joe Biden has reached 1,991 delegates and has won the nomination for what is his third bid to become President of the United States of America. The race to the White House begins amid a pandemic spiralling out of control, racial and social injustices, economic disaster, and unemployment on a massive scale. The President and the nominee disagree on almost every issue and now it looks like the Presidential Election will, at least in part, be run on mail-in votes or online. This raises the question of Cyber Crime. Indeed, this is one of President's Trump's main objections to the move away from in-person voting.

With the election now less than 150 days away many fear the move to mail votes leaves room for cyber-attacks and results being interfered with. Specifically, the threat seems to come from Vladimir Putin of Russia. Trump claims it invites fraud and favours the Democrats when in fact it is unlikely to favour either party. But it does provoke larger turnout or more votes. The Department of Homeland Security views the move to online and mail-in voting as high risk. Online state voter registration processes, records, and systems were chief targets of Russian hackers in 2016. Both parties and the American people are worried of the consequences if this happens again. In 2016 data was not actually interfered with but it proved that it is possible to access data and therefore cast doubt on the validity of any election result. The Russian's don't actually have to change data as knowing they could do it is enough to derail the whole process. Last summer the Department of Homeland Security hired Rand Corporation to evaluate the nation's vulnerable election areas. It was found that State and local databases could be locked by hackers and ransoms demanded. Or results could be manipulated. Towns, counties, and States are urged to back up their systems and have paper copy in case the digital platforms are rendered inaccessible.

The Director of Homeland Security Cyber Systems and Infrastructure Security Agency is Christopher C Krebbs. He indicates intense focus on hardening registration systems is vital. Teams are working to make sure that towns, cities, counties, and States plug software vulnerabilities and back up their systems and have paper print out of poll books to assist if criminals or other nations adversely interfere on election day. Rand Corporation was hired to evaluate the nation's vulnerabilities in registering and voting and findings fuelled existing fear that Government and State databases are vulnerable. As more and more States rush to accommodate mail and online voting, chaos ensues and courts are increasingly called to help. Mr Krebbs is further concerned about the internet voting platform used in Delaware and West Virginia as it is open to ballots being manipulated at large scale and that the hackers could go undetected. One platform already in use for internet and remote voting can be manipulated after the votes are cast and not even be detected by the company who owns the platform. The platform, called Omni ballot, was in fact used last week for the Delaware Primary and West Virginia. Colorado plans to use it in November while New Jersey has trialled it in local elections last month. Various jurisdictions in Colorado, Florida, Oregon, Ohio, and Washington use the platform as a way for voters to mark ballots remotely and submit by email, fax, or mail. Both uses of the system presented opportunities for hackers. The chief executive of the platform, Bryan Finney, defended it, saying it was serving voters well before the pandemic. Now, however, as nearly every State moves to online/mail voting for November 3rd, it is clear problems must be resolved. The platform owners say new upgrades are full proof. In the rush there are of course legal and legislative matters to attend to. Some states are having difficulty getting the correct laws in place and meeting the various requirements. For example, in Texas, the Supreme Court blocked the expansion of mail ballots. But in Ohio lawmakers approved a Republican bill that makes voting by mail more difficult, removing prepaid postage and cutting in half the time to request an absentee ballot. In Tennessee, the Republican Secretary of State pledged to fight a court ruling that would allow mail voting across the State.

In addition, officials warn the threat of Russian interference in the election voting system is very real. Google believes Chinese hackers were targeting email accounts of campaign staff working for Joe Biden. Google further suggests Iran has targeted Trump's campaign. Trump continues to dismiss all of this and maintains his opposition to the plan as he says mail votes favour the Democrats, even though a paper trail can prove validity. It remains to be seen what havoc hackers cause between now and the election and what is done to prevent it. But the ongoing threat and fears of many calls into question perhaps the validity of any result and even if the President accepts it. [20]

Edging into the middle of June and following George Floyd's funeral in Houston, it is difficult to remember sometimes that this is election year. Demonstrations dominate news alongside the ever-growing pandemic, economy, and healthcare problems in the country. Facebook is fast becoming the chosen platform for campaign profiles with Joe Biden spending $2 million on advertising. Usually with photographs of President Trump and slamming his actions in every area. Conversely the Trump camp takes the opposite direction and spends $120,000 on ads denouncing the riots, and even claiming they are the actions of far-left activist groups and just opportunists. This is

---

[20] Extract from New York Times; Mark Makela, David E Sanger, Nicole Pelroth, Matthew Rosenberg.

unsubstantiated. He also spent $40,000 trying to discredit an organisation he calls "Antifa" which he claims, wrongly, co-ordinate the looting and violent protests. [21]

> *To me, it seems both campaigns are just mudslinging rather than engaging in action campaigning and putting forward agendas for the way forward. I find it very sad that the dignity which should exist in this process is lacking. But it is the same in British politics. The Brexit talks are almost lost, however, at home among the Covid-19 public health crisis.*

As voting begins in Georgia today, 10th June, long lines of queuing voters and problems with voting machines, it appears that Joe Biden is in a stronger position to remove the incumbent President from office than any challenge since Bill Clinton in 1992.[22]

Still in the aftermath of the killing and subsequent funeral of George Floyd, the talk continues to focus on reform, The Black Lives Matter movement, and a move to rename Confederate Army bases where links to past slavery and historic figures involved in slavery dominates. President Trump is opposed to renaming Army bases. Joe Biden positions himself more sympathetically. While the virus spread appears to be slowing, both sides of Congress turn attention elsewhere with Trump appearing ready to hit the campaign trail and The White House announce his first rally to be in Tulsa on 19th June. The date is an unfortunate choice which he later changes as it is unofficially called "Juneteenth." A date which celebrates the African American freedom from slavery and Tulsa is also the site of possibly the most violent and destructive white mob-violence against African Americans in the 20th century and is 99 years ago this month.

Difficulties of mail and online voting plague both campaigns and while the President opposes it he is seen sitting in his Oval Office writing his own mail-in vote for a Primary. Joe Biden counters by

---

[21] New York Times On Politics.
[22] New York Times; Nate Cohen.

saying his party will put in a major initiative with lawyers to make sure every district in the country is patrolled and that voting will be secure. Joe Biden talks of police reform rather than the calls which abound to "defund the police" and would look at more leniency in law enforcement and emphasise rehab, not prison, particularly in drug-related crimes. Where Trump in 2016 was seen as the lesser of two evils the same could well be happening in 2020. Neither the floundering President nor the Democratic nominee are commanding confidence from voters. Swing States, as before, are the key.

However, slightly more views are held this year in relation to the handling of the pandemic and this, rather than policy, may define the eventual outcome, in my opinion.

Much of Joe Biden's negative press came from fellow competitors for the nomination but as they dropped out of the race one by one his popularity seems to have risen. Mid-June, a high-quality poll sees 45 percent positive and 46 percent negative for Biden. Liberals are least likely to support him. For Trump, most conservatives see him in a favourable light. Young people view both contenders in a poor light. Maybe the question is does an unhappy Republican vote for Joe Biden?

Following Juneteenth celebrations, Trump goes ahead with the Tulsa rally. His first since March 2nd and he is currently trailing Joe Biden in the polls. Oklahoma has one of the lowest infection rates and while social distancing is encouraged in the crowds it is still a risky exercise. People must buy tickets and sign a disclaimer that if they contract the virus at the event the President's campaign is not responsible for any illness or injury.[23]

---

[23] BBC News for US and Canada.

CHAPTER 19

Campaigns and More Covid

By contrast Joe Biden's rally in Philadelphia in the same week looks a little different. Such events are normally all-singing-all-dancing loud affairs with music, crowds, handshaking, and fanfare. This time about 20 handpicked officials with folding chairs socially distanced in the room. No line up for candidates to pose for selfies, no music. Everyone had their temperature tested on arrival and all were required to wear a mask. Joe Biden's own arrival with no fanfare was very low key apart from the lectern being adorned with the banner loudly declaring "REOPEN RIGHT: SAFER AND STRONGER." In opening words, he proceeded to rip through the President's actions, highlighting his failure to effectively fight the Coronavirus and highlighting also that Trump said in March "it will go away" and followed it up with more similar Tweets in April. [24]

Polls currently seem to indicate that Joe Biden's choice of running mate is a factor in the success of his campaign and the continuing momentum and eagerness among Democrats for him to choose, as he pledged earlier this year, a female, black African/American is the popular consensus so far. Trump's rally in Tulsa drew smaller crowds than expected and rumours flew around that young voters launched a social media campaign which allegedly encouraged people to buy tickets and then not turn up in a bid to have all the empty seats we saw on the day. The anticipated

---

[24] New York Times; Lisa Lerer; On Politics.

crowd of 19,000 was definitely not the case and the plan to broadcast to more thousands outsides was cancelled. It is suspected that many of those behind the alleged social media campaign are too young to vote but if it is true then they have had their say. Worse news for Trump at the rally is that as White House staffers arrived to set up, six were found to test positive for Coronavirus and sent off to quarantine.

Now, as of 21st June, there are 2.2 million Coronavirus cases and 119,00 deaths in the US.

Just as Biden had taken swipes at Trump in Philadelphia, President Trump threw his own rhetoric at Biden, calling him "a helpless puppet of the radical left." Further criticism followed when referring to the toppling of statues in the wake of the killing of George Floyd, anti-racism demonstrations saying "the unhinged left-wing mob is trying to vandalise our history … and persecute anyone who does not conform to their demands for absolute and total control. We are not conforming." Clear enough.

Looking ahead to the Primaries of New York and Kentucky, the moving tapestry of the pandemic and economic crisis is a challenge for anyone. Maybe bolder and more aggressive approaches in political campaigns now are called for. The request for absentee ballots is soaring and in-person voting is limited. Long lines due to social distancing measures will form and results will take days to be confirmed.

From today 23rd June the On Politics section of the *New York Times* is publishing a series of new polls looking at the race for Presidency between Trump and Biden, will focus on battleground States, how the voters feel, and the mood of the country. The first such poll reports that Joe Biden leads President Trump by 14 points. An unpopular President falling further as the crisis continues. 58% of voters disapprove of his handling of the crisis, and only 38% approved. In almost every subgroup Biden either leads or matches Trump and Biden has apparently gained a greater advantage than in 2016 among independents such as perhaps college-educated white women. Among men and women who are usually Republican Biden is equal with Trump. Where Trump provokes a love or hate feeling, Joe Biden attracts less extreme feelings among voters.

President Trump's rally in Tulsa and a further one in Phoenix followed similar formats and similar rhetoric in attacking what he laments as Joe Biden's failings and shortcomings, in my opinion. His 2016 campaign at this point was loudly promoting what he would change in America and promises of making America great. So far, mostly silent, Joe Biden has not pushed his campaign policy, goals, or visions either. The virus is still ripping through Southern and Western States and both candidates' attention is on that for now, perhaps. But Joe Biden is looking, at this point, like the popular choice among voters against an increasingly unpopular President.[25]

The NYT/Siena college poll reporting on 25th June a poll of six battleground States that clinched Trump's victory in 2016 shows that his once solid lead among white voters has all but vanished. If it stays that way he would not be re-elected. Joe Biden would win with at least 333 electoral votes if he won all six of the states surveyed and those held by Clinton. The poll further suggests that Trump's deteriorating position could threaten his Republican Senate majority, possibly in Arizona, North Carolina, and hitting Republican hopes in Michigan. A point of note here is that the Republican Senate seems to have pushed the bench to the right since 2017 and this week Trump announced the 200th judge of his term in office.

The early pointers in the Kentucky and New York primaries indicate progressive voters in African/American, Latino voters combined are faring well. While results are pending, President Trump's political landscape is further damaged when it is reported that three months ago he was briefed on alleged interference from Russia in Afghanistan in that cash was found in US$. Captured

---

[25] New York Times. Campaign reporting.

and interrogated militia claimed it was a cash bounty for US soldiers lives. The Democrats are outraged, with Joe Biden launching into an attack at a virtual Town Hall meeting that "his (Trump) entire presidency has become a gift to Putin, but this is beyond the pale ... it's a betrayal of the most sacred duty we bear as a Nation to protect and equip our troops when we send them into harm's way!" [26]

Cash Bounty for US Soldiers and Russia

Since last January intelligence and special ops have reported their suspicions that Russia is offering payment to Taliban fighters to kill US troops and target US bases in Afghanistan.

With events still evolving almost hourly as the Pandemic holds fast on the path of destructionm I am going to report the daily brief as a weekly summary while trying to keep on top of the Democratic Primary results. We are all being dominated by Coronavirus, but the election must go on, as must Brexit for the UK. Hard to believe just how much there is to do, how much sorrow and death is ever present in our daily lives. I am not sure how to limit the daily brief as leaving anything out, wherever in the world it is happening, seems wrong or even unfair so I hope when reading this you stick with it, overwhelming as it may feel.

DB 1st to 8th July 2020

❏ At the beginning of the first week in July in the US, Dr Anthony Fauci raises his concerns again at the rising number of cases, now standing at 47,000 reported in one day in the United States. The US Centre for Disease Control and Prevention

---

[26] New York Times.

calls this discouraging and 15 States pull back on reopening measures. Earlier signs of economic recovery are in reverse now in Arizona and Texas. The week ends with the view that the US is still in the first wave of the pandemic with 250,000 cases announced this week and the total deaths in the US now passes 130,000.

- Europe continues with reopening measures but places a ban on travellers from the US, Russia, and Brazil where cases are surging. Travellers from Australia and Canada are permitted into Europe, as is China if they reciprocate.
- The referendum on 1st July in Russia looks set to fall Putin's way and will keep him in power until 2036 if agreed.
- A new strain of swine flu is discovered in China relating to pig farms thought to have pandemic possibilities.
- Putin was indeed successful in the referendum yesterday and will remain in power until 2036.
- In Spain, while reopening continues, Catalonia has imposed lockdown again amid surging cases.
- England drops the mandatory 14-day quarantine for visitors from more than 50 countries from 10th July.
- Britain announces the first sanctions of a post-Brexit Britain with dozens affecting Russia, Saudi Arabia, Myanmar being blacklisted for past abuses such as assassinations and persecutions. Many of these are already blacklisted by the US.

CHAPTER 20

Primary Standings and the Way Forward

In a televised speech Joe Biden surprises the President by accusing him of failing on every level to confront the virus and again highlighting that in March he (Biden) recommended increasing federal support for testing, tracing, PPE supplies, vaccine research, and national stands for reopening the economy. The speech came as cases surged. President Trump denies all knowledge of the dollars to the Russians for US soldiers' lives.

Further Primary results are recorded as:

Kentucky, Joe Biden 52.

New York State, Joe Biden 164.

Ohio, Joe Biden 115.

As fear surrounds in-person voting, the demand for absentee ballots grows and now 41 States allow people to vote online, but only 18 States allow voters to request absentee ballots online. In other states a cumbersome process of mailing requests in and visiting an election office to complete applications persists. In 13 of the States not offering an online absentee ballot request it is possible to print one, sign at home, and scan or fax it back. [27]

Wisconsin, a known swing State which looks to be going to Joe Biden this year, saw two court decisions this week, one favouring

---

[27] Brennan Centre for Justice.

Democrat and the other pleasing the Republicans. A move to purge the voters roll of potential out-of-date registrations was settled by the Supreme Court who ruled against it and it will likely not happen now until after the 3rd of November elections, which the Democrats welcomed. However, on Monday last (29th June) a decision handed down by three judges appointed by a Republican President, by a federal appeals court on multiple voting laws and regulations which had been pending for years left the Democrats dismayed. The early-vote period will be two weeks, not six as in 2016, absentee ballots must be mailed not emailed or faxed and voters must have resided in their current home for 28 days, not 10 days as before, in order to vote. The appeals court did however allow that a student with out-of-date ID may vote if they prove they tried to get a valid ID. If no ID available they need an affidavit proving application for one. This legal wrangling has taken a year.

4th July

This year celebrations are very muted with many beaches, cafes, bars, and restaurants remaining closed and American people not feeling much like celebrating at all.

Both Trump and Biden announce their campaign fundraising totals with Biden raising $141 million and Trump $131 million. The Trump campaign has around $295 million banked which is a lot more than Biden. President Trump moves to put the Black Lives Matter into his campaign but tweets that he would veto a bill to fund the military if it included provision to remove Confederate leaders' names from US military bases. The row over "defunding the police" continues. The consensus seems to be that reform is needed, however, and most Americans now understand it is not to eliminate peacekeepers but to look at alternative ways to maintain law and order. President Trump announces his desire to create a National Garden of American Heroes. He signs an executive order to establish a suitable task force to this end and states it must include all historical figures, even controversial ones.

The Supreme Court ruled unanimously on 6th July that States could bar faithless electors. If, for example, Colorado chose a Democrat for President the Electoral College can require members to vote for said Democrat. It may stop members going awry but has anomalies and consequences. If electors can be required to vote with the State's popular vote, could that apply nationally? Probably not but the ruling left a grey area which no doubt needs looking into.[28]

DB 8th to 15th July

- President Trump pushes for all schools to open in the fall. He said safety guidelines set out by the US disease control agency are too tough and too expensive. Mike Pense offers that the agency issue new guidelines. Trump further threatens to cut funding for schools who don't comply with the return orders. On higher education the Trump administration says it will strip international students of their Visas if their college hold classes entirely online, prompting Harvard and Massachusetts Institute of Technology to sue to block the directive. President Trump, having previously avoided wearing a mask, turned up on a visit to the Walter Reid Centre, visiting veterans and health workers, and now says wearing a mask could be a good thing.

- The US is still recording the highest number of new cases in the world and on 9th July alone seeing 59,460 new cases reported. Hospitals across the South and West are being overwhelmed.

- It comes to light that a doctor working in the emergency room in Manhattan became so affected by her hospital being

---

[28] New York Times; OnPolitics.

overwhelmed and feeling so helpless and unable to save lives that she tragically suffered a breakdown and in April Dr Lorna Breem took her own life.

❏ Britain's announcement to ban using Huawei technology (see below) on 14th July is seen by Trump as a victory after some tense phone calls between him and Boris Johnson. Post-Brexit trade talks are very much in both men's minds perhaps. At the time of the announcement President Trump's National security advisor is in Paris having meetings about China with representatives from Britain, France, Germany, and Italy.

❏ Also, President Trump reverses his decision of 6th July to strip foreign students of their visas if their colleges present learning and teaching online in the fall. Many Colleges and Universities launched court cases in objection.

❏ The 15th of July sees talk of the Trump administration issuing orders seeking to tighten White House control over the Coronavirus information on cases, deaths, hospital admissions, intensive care etc by asking for all information to be sent to the H.H.S instead of as currently the C.D.C. Many object, calling for the current process to continue.

❏ Sweden, who avoided full lockdown and tried to protect the economy and jobs, are seeing little gain for their strategy. In fact, they have recorded thousands more deaths than their neighbours of Norway and Denmark but suffered similar economic downturn. Sweden has to date, 8th July, lost 5,420 lives to Covid-19. Per million of the population Sweden has lost 40 percent more than the US, 12 times more than Norway, seven times more than Finland, and six times more than Denmark.

❏ Hong Kong enters a third wave of the virus with 38 new infections on the 8th of July as Japan bans screaming on roller coaster rides to help stop spread.

- Britain's Chancellor of the Exchequer (9th July) announces his summer budget with £38 billion to boost the economy and save jobs. The economy shrank 25 percent in two months after taking 18 years to reach pre pre-pandemic position.
- Scotland's first minister announces the gradual path into phase three of easing lockdown, allowing larger outdoor groups of households, indoor visitors (limited), indoor dining in pubs and bars, and hairdressers will open on 15th July.
- Globally there are now 12 million confirmed cases of Covid-19 and 549,000 deaths. 9th July 2020.
- Protestors in Russia shout "Putin resign" on Saturday (11th) as they call for the release of a popular regional governor who was arrested last week on suspicion of multiple murders.
- In the UK, while reopening in England is moving faster than the other three nations, it is announced on 13th July that in Herefordshire 200 farm workers are placed in self-isolation after 73 of them tested positive for Covid-19. They are mostly asymptomatic, workers flown in from the EU and are picking and packing beans and broccoli. The Public Health England is supporting the farm, near Malvern in Worcestershire, and says the spread of the virus through food is unlikely.
- The news on 14th July from the UK is Boris Johnson announcing Britain's ban on equipment from the Chinese telecommunications firm Huawei. While Boris Johnson may have given way to pressure from President Trump, it does signal a willingness from Western countries to confront China.
- And in bad news for Britain, it is said the economy, which was hoped to grow by 5.5 percent in the early reopening phase. grew just 1.8 percent. Better news across Europe though as many go on a spending spree.

CHAPTER 21

President Trump's Finances, Supreme Court Rulings, and Roger Stone

Donald Trump suffers another blow as the Supreme Court of Justice rule to allow prosecutors to see his financial records. A second ruling denies records to congress however and only prosecutors in New York will have visibility for now. Public viewing is likely to be only after the election. Health officials comment that his rally held in Tulsa last month likely contributed to around 500 new Coronavirus cases in the area. The President's niece, Mary L Trump, daughter of his elder brother Fred who died aged just 42 after a battle with alcoholism, publishes a book set to cause the President further grief privately and perhaps publicly. *The book is very unflattering and will no doubt cause a stir.*[29]

Joe Biden's allies and backers of Bernie Sanders have been looking at policy issues for the campaign. The task force, looking to attract left-wing young voters, sent recommendations to the Joe Biden campaign staffers on 8th July. Proposals support the aim of adding a public option to the Affordable Care for All Act rather than Medicare for All. The education taskforce didn't co-sign making public college tuition free for all, nor cancelling student debt. They called for an end to power plant emissions by 2035 and recommended barring federal contracts with companies paying less than $15 per hour to workers or who undermine

---

[29] Belfast Telegraph.

unionisation efforts.[30]

9th July sees the Supreme Court reject President Trump's claim that he cannot be investigated while in office. Details above included in the daily brief.

The On Politics in *New York Times* writes today (13th July) that two weeks ago the same chief Justice John Roberts joined with four liberal jurists in ruling that workplace discrimination against L.G.B.T.Q is unconstitutional, announced from the same court a ruling of seven to two decisions the other way. One allows religious employers to fire people on grounds that are otherwise considered discriminatory. The other ruling permits the Trump administration to let employers with religious or moral objections deny their workers birth control coverage. Chief Justice John Roberts is a conservative appointed by a Republican President. In further controversy for the Republican camp, President Trump announces on Friday 11th July that he will commute the sentence of his friend and former advisor, Roger Stone, convicted of seven felonies and had been sentenced to 40 months in prison. Among critics are Mitt Romney who tweeted "unprecedented, historic corruption: an American President commutes the sentence of a person convicted by a jury of lying to shield that very President." Pat Toomey is also critical but simply offers the view that commuting the sentence is a mistake. Trump fired back on Twitter, calling them both RINOS (Republican in name only).

---

[30] New York Times; On Politics.

CHAPTER 22

16 Weeks Until Election Day!

On 14th July, the picture for Donald Trump is looking like a tough landscape with Coronavirus cases surging within Florida, the site of the Republican Convention next month, putting it in a dire situation as the epicentre of the virus with many Republicans saying they will not attend. Jeff Sessions is trailing in the Alabama polls while reckoning his campaign is on track and the Texas Supreme Court rules against the State Republican Party holding an in-person convention. 17 States are now suing over the move to strip foreign students of visas where colleges and universities present online teaching. And to top it off, a new poll shows Joe Biden leading in Texas. A Dallas Morning News/University of Texas poll finds Joe Biden with a five-point lead. In April, a similar poll suggested a tie at 43 percent each. If a Democratic Presidential candidate wins in Texas in November then that will be the first time since former President Carter in 1976. By 15th July in Florida the situation grows ever worse and the planned convention in Jacksonville will most likely move to an outdoor event. Masks and strict hygiene measures will be in place. Ironic as President Trump moved to the Florida location as he objected to the Democratic Governor's view that if held in Charlotte, North Carolina, as originally planned, then masks would be mandatory. Rounding off this seven-day period, Joe Biden, during a speech to reporters yesterday in Wilmington, unveiled a $2 trillion plan to fight climate change. Plans put forward to eliminate fossil fuel by 2050 and to be clean air reliant in the US by then. While not endorsing a previous plan by Bernie Sanders, Alexandra-Ocasio Cortez, and other progressive leaders known as The Green New Deal, much of his plan is within this scope. However, it is viewed by some as progressive and visionary while President Trump denounced it as extreme and further saying Biden "is embracing The Green New Deal and other socialist priorities that will devastate American families and business."[31]

DB 16th to 23rd July

- In a bizarre happening it seems that Kanye West wishes to run for President, along with 1,144 other people.
- Late on the 16th of July a new poll suggests voters are losing faith in the incumbent President's handling of the economy and that Joe Biden leads by 15 points over Trump. Credit; Sky News, Russell Hope.
- Britain has evidence to support the theory that Black and ethnic minority women are being hardest hit by the pandemic. Many have lost jobs and, as they tend to be low paid, or they have lost more than one job, they are especially hard hit. It is also likely that they do not qualify for any government support scheme.
- The crisis is hitting many States hard and because back in April the White House moved responsibility to State governors, many States differ in how it is handled, and many see this as a mistake and lack of leadership from the President.
- It was reported on the 18th of July that John Lewis died on Friday 17th, aged 80. He co-founded the Student Nonviolent Co-ordinating committee and helped organise the 1963 march in Washington and eventually became an activist as he had promised and served in Congress for 30 years. While tributes

---

[31] New York Times; On Politics.

flood in, President Trump simply issues a terse statement of condolences.

❏ In the ABC News/Washington poll, Biden is shown to lead Trump by 15 points and Biden showing a good average lead over the last month.

❏ The US announced on the 23rd a $2 billion contract with German biotechnology company Pfizer for 100 million Coronavirus vaccines. Not yet proven but in development and showing positive results in trials.

❏ The US has reached four million cases, but the President blames the rise in part to more testing. It is also thought that actual cases could be 13 times more as only positive tests are recorded while many people have mild symptoms and don't get tested.

❏ In light of the surge in Florida, the President cancels the Republican National Convention event due to take place in Jacksonville next month. Many Republicans had already said they would not go anyway.

❏ News comes out on the 16th/17th July that America, Canada, and Britain have been hit by Russian hackers. It seems they seek to access data on the Coronavirus vaccine to try and speed up their own efforts in finding one rather than to destroy or interfere with data. The Oxford University and a British/Swedish firm Astra/Zeneca said no data was stolen although they detected hackers as far back as February.

❏ The British Prime Minister, Boris Johnson, held a briefing setting out his plan and thoughts on easing current lockdown restrictions further over the next nine months and his plans for government support if a second wave of the virus hits over winter.

❏ Two socially distant and significant Royal events took place in Windsor today (July 17th). Her Majesty the Queen along with Prince Philip, Duke of Edinburgh, attended the wedding of Princess Beatrice, daughter of beleaguered Prince Andrew and

Sarah Ferguson, Duchess of York, in a private ceremony attended by just 30 people. Later in the afternoon, her Majesty knighted Captain Tom Moore who raised over £32 million for charity by walking laps of his garden 100 times before his 100th birthday. The investiture was held outside in the gardens of Windsor Castle with just Captain Sir Thomas Moore, his daughter, son-in-law, and two grandchildren. The Queen had two Equerry with her, and a Piper played. Credit; BBC News.

- In Britain by 20th July Boris Johnson announces an investigation into the handling of the Pandemic on every level and it is initially thought that if he had imposed lockdown one week earlier it could have saved 30,000 lives.

- The European Union finally agrees to the terms of the 7.5 billion Euros package deal to help the member states recover from the pandemic, headed up by Angela Merkel of Germany and Emmanuel Macron of France. (Britain, who has left the EU, continues Brexit and trade talks.)

- News on the 21st of progress on a vaccine in Britain is welcomed. Two potential vaccines have positive results from Oxford University and also Chinese company Cansino.

- Meanwhile, the UK suspends its extradition treaty with Hong Kong, Britain, and Russia.

- A report by British parliamentary committee looking at Russian interference in the country's affairs is issued and shows many areas where previous interference was evident, including the country's EU referendum. Although there is no proof of this, there is a clear sign of interference in the independence referendum of 2014 which would have seen Scotland leave the Union.

- Russian money has been flooding into London for many years as the Capital welcomed Oligarchs and was subsequently dubbed "Londongrad." There is growing concern at the clear indication that Russia has Britain as a primary target.

- At the same time (21st), the agreed rescue deal in the European Union sees the Dutch Prime Minister and his equal part in Austria form a block of smaller countries (known as the "frugals") to try and restrain the spending ambitions of France and poorer countries in the South.
- World Coronavirus statistics; 15 million confirmed cases. 617,000 deaths.
- US Coronavirus statistics; 3.97 million confirmed cases. 144,000 deaths.[32]
- It is reported on 23rd that China vows to retaliate as the US orders Beijing to close their consulate office in Houston, Texas. There are rising suspicions of cybercrime coming from China and Russia and of course China denies this.
- At the daily briefing, the First Minister of Scotland Nicola Sturgeon announced on 23rd that from tomorrow (Friday 24th), those shielding will be able to now meet up with two households indoors and up to eight people, or four households outdoors and up to 15 people. Also, citizens are now able to visit shops, bars, and restaurants.

However, for many people (myself included) the prospect of going out in society while risk exists, albeit very small now, is quite daunting. But I was able to visit my elderly mother who lives some distance away and is very ill, for the first time in five months. Joyous for both of us.

---

[32] Multimedia sources.

CHAPTER 23

Shifting Landscapes as Conventions Approach

President Trump's campaign at the moment consists of news conferences in the Rose Garden of the White House where he criticizes Joe Biden, compliments himself on the creation of a "garden of statues" as the new "big, beautiful wall" and offers nothing by way of hope or promise for the next four years should he stay in office. Saying that Joe Biden lacks "strength and stamina" to be President is maybe not enough for the American people. The people seem to feel that the country is sinking and are looking for leadership. On the other track is Joe Biden who is benefitting from the falling trust in the current government. Most governors are ignoring federal advice and directives and trying to cope with the crisis in their own States as they wish to do. Joe Biden released an ad in Texas reinforcing wearing a mask, washing hands, and social distancing measures with a rallying call of all being in it together. This should have come from the government leading the country and yet the top story is the Pandemic with Trump's campaign coming in second place. [33]

Mitt Romney, Larry Hogan, and Liz Cheney, descendants of Republicans of note from the past, all cast dissenting voices on the President. Gov Larry Hogan of Maryland has been a leading voice of frustration at Trump's handling of the crisis. Liz Cheney is

---

[33] New York Times; On Politics.

the most persistent critic of the Trump administration security plan.[34] Credit; Washington, Mark Leibovic.

With Trump constantly doing no more than criticizing Joe Biden, will that present an opportunity in Ohio for Biden? Where it was once all uphill, the Democratic nominee is now gaining ground.

President Trump is portraying some tension between himself Dr Fauci and some Republicans have also turned against the medic, but in the young and independent Democrats the reverse is happening, and trust has risen to the point of 86 percent of Democrats and two thirds of independents having faith in him, according to a Quinnipiac poll. Overall, the same poll indicates 65 percent belief in Dr Fauci. [35]

President Trump garners more negative press as he sends in military-clad federal agents to patrol the streets in Portland, Oregon, who subsequently turn tear gas on demonstrators and throw them into vans with no explanation or order. This is probably the shape of things to come as he considers doing it in other States seeing demonstrations. The State Attorney files a lawsuit accusing the federal agents of unlawful tactics. Trump, who has previously signed an executive order directing federal agencies to protect monuments and statues, said on Fox News Sunday that the protestors are "anarchists." Trump's falling popularity is again clarified in two polls over the same weekend by ABC/Washington that Americans trust Joe Biden 20 percent more than they trust Donald Trump to handle the pandemic. And 56 percent of voters said they disapprove of the current handling of the pandemic by the President. Conversely, most Americans see Dr Fauci favourably with 44 percent offering strong support.

Passion for voting for anyone at the moment is not huge in either camp with Joe Biden looking at just 39 percent of voters enthusiasm and 69 percent (Republican) passionate about voting for Trump. But the top and dominating story is and will be the

---

[34] Washington, Mark Leibovic.
[35] New York Times; On Politics.

Pandemic. Cybercrime issues flow into the mix with California rejecting mail-in ballots, Trump's opposition to expanding access to mail-in voting, seeking to restrict funding for the postal service and blocking funds to improve election administration. It has been suggested that if Biden wins then President Trump could refuse to accept the result and he himself is non-committal on that score. Joe Biden has now led the incumbent President by an average of eight points in polls over the last month. This represents the highest and longest lead of any previous candidate for the Presidency, and all by just making occasional appearances on the campaign trail. [36]

In a speech (21st July) near his home in Delaware, Joe Biden floated a plan to spend $775 billion on an initiative to create jobs for caregivers, and better affordable home and health care access, especially for those on Medicare and the 800,000 on a waiting list for home and community care. The proposal seeks to fund 150,00 new jobs, end the waiting list, and give tax breaks as well as help the unofficial carers who look after a relative and cannot work because of this.

Negotiations with House Democrats by the Republicans on the next stage of Coronavirus legislation kicks off but is now likely to run into August so any expanded unemployment insurance will expire before the new bill is passed. Republicans seek $100 billion of funding for schools and small business loan programmes. Trump previously insisted that education funds were to be tied to in-person teaching by all schools and colleges in the fall and it is unclear if this is still the case. In another unpopular move, Trump vows to send federal agents into cities to deal with demonstrations but also now to deal with violent crime in Chicago which sits dubiously outside the executive order he signed to "protect monuments and statues."[37]

The Trump campaign is thought to have spent $20 million over the

---

[36] New York Times.
[37] New York Times.

last 20 days on TV adverts focused solely on the issue of the police force. Joe Biden is focussing on investing in tax enforcement on the wealthy which is also part of his $775 billion plan to help caregivers and working parents. [38]

DB 24th to 31st July

Sunday the 25th of July sees a major fundraising event hosted on Zoom by Joe Biden and includes many celebrities and party faithful who have paid top dollar to join in the event and support the campaign. During the last week of July, it will be worth looking at the amount of money raised in Donald Trump's campaign and then Joe Biden as there are now around 100 days until election day. It is also worth noting this week's figures surrounding the Coronavirus pandemic and how each presidential candidate tackles the ongoing problem while campaigning. [39]

- Over the weekend of 25th and 26th July protesters continued to clash with federal agents in Portland, Oregon, and in Seattle, as protests continue across many cities. Around 5,000 people were dealt with by federal agents where some of them were setting fires.
- 26th July, Joe Biden's virtual streaming fundraiser hosted and attended by many high-profile campaign support chairs and headlined with John Legend and Andra Day performing their duet of Whitney Houston's hit "Greatest Love of All."
- By 28th July, the White House confirms that Robert O'Brien, National Security Advisor to Trump, has tested positive with Covid-19 but is suffering mild symptoms so far. While he works in the West Wing close to the Oval Office, it is believed his last close contact with the President was two weeks ago. He

---

[38] New York Times. On Politics.
[39] Sally Foster.

recently made a trip to Europe meeting with officials from other countries for talks followed by a short family holiday when he was indeed caught on video not social distancing nor wearing a mask. Credit CNN.

- The US sets out plans to withdraw around 12 thousand troops from Germany and relocate them to Belgium and Italy while some will return to the US. The defence secretary announced this on Wednesday.

- In news from around the world, Russia also sees rallies. Many are protesting against the previous arrests of a popular governor. Putin, who, after a referendum, voted to keep him in power until 2036, faces unrest from many of the people but it is thought that an alternative to Putin would be worse and he holds on to around 60% popularity in recent polls.

- Meanwhile in Europe the British government announces on Sunday 26th that all travellers returning from Spain must now quarantine for 14 days after Covid-19 cases rise significantly in Spain. The tourist industry is in dismay after being hard hit by the pandemic and travellers face many problems on their return home, including the possibility of not being paid while they quarantine.

- In Scotland Nicola Sturgeon, the First Minister, announces that all school children will return as normal on 11th August but that teaching staff and all other adults must socially distance of two meters. Parents and unions are concerned. She also said that shielding, which almost two million have followed since 23rd March, can be paused from 1st August. Good news for me. However, it simply means the risk is lower than it was and all in Scotland now follow phase three of the route map out of lockdown. The virus is still live and although at a minimum level there are small outbreaks in local clusters. Also, the advice changes regarding self-isolation from seven days if you have symptoms to 10 days and warning that 14-day quarantine may be imposed on travellers coming to Scotland from other European countries including Germany, Belgium, and France.

❏ Rounding off the week, the UK Prime Minister Boris Johnson holds back from more lockdown easing from tomorrow due to rising daily cases and outbreaks in three large parts of England. Stricter measures re-imposed and people advised not to travel cross border unless essential. Chief Medical officer Chris Whitty says Britain or England in this case has reached the limit of lockdown easing while controlling the spread of the virus.

❏ Further Russian interference is reported on 29th July. The US intelligence accuses the G.R.U., Russian intelligence agency, of putting out false information with a false report of Chinese arguing that the virus was created by the American military. The data was published on InfoRos, a site controlled by the Russian government and also on a small independent site, Oneworld.press, which officials say has ties to the G.R.U. The intention of messing with the Presidential election is more and more evident.

❏ Belarus accuses Russia of interfering with their presidential election, saying about 200 mercenaries had infiltrated the country disguised as tourists. This report is not confirmed. Grim news from the US, particularly for President Trump, as the G.D.P fell by 9.5 percent in the first three months to June, being the largest quarterly drop on record.

❏ Virus death toll hits 150,000 and Trump still trails in the polls. Waiting for the announcement of the VP to Joe Biden.

❏ And the funeral of John Lewis takes place in Atlanta with former President Barack Obama delivering a powerful eulogy while Mr Trump declines to attend. Almost in desperation Trump reiterates that he could delay the election amid accusations that it will be corrupt due to cyber interference.

CHAPTER 24

When Does a Campaign Begin?

With just one primary left (Connecticut) on 11th August and 100 days to go until election day, the Biden campaign is poised for a push into the fall and while Trump tries to shift his focus from the Coronavirus to crime and Republicans frantically try to reschedule the cancelled Florida RNC, Joe Biden kicks off a virtual high-profile fundraiser, live streaming on Sunday 26th July. Credit; ABC News. 100 days after Bernie Sanders dropped out of the race as Presidential candidate, the Biden fundraiser goes out with John Legend and Andra Day performing a duet and attended by Barbara Streisand, Kamala Harris, and a host of high-profile supporters. Due to the pandemic, the push for Joe Biden's camp in the campaign is now almost entirely virtual with some 500 events planned across the States. He will be pushing hard to highlight Donald Trump's shortcomings in the handling of the pandemic, the turbulent economic fallout, and pushing even harder his own agenda and spending plans. He holds onto his lead in the polls. [40]

Running Mate Musings

With August fast approaching, Joe Biden promises to announce his running mate by the first week in August. He is likely to follow

---

[40] ABC News; Mike Memoli.

up on his promise to choose a female African American from a list of names previously noted to include Elizabeth Warren, Kamala Harris, and also a recent contender, Susan Rice. Late considerations in the running are Senator Tammy Duckworth of Illinois and Representative Karen Bass of California. Joe Biden made this promise after giving a speech outlining his economic plan, titled "Build Back Better". This plan includes proposals to address racial inequalities embedded in the United States' economy. Joe Biden continues to focus his energies on the traditional democratic values and helping the Black and Brown communities.[41]

Looking at the Dollars

Nearing the end of July, with less than 100 days until election day, the focus for both candidates is narrowing and spending on TV ads is ramping up from both campaigns. Florida, a key State, is being swamped by ads. There has been big spending from the Trump camp with $17.2 million spent there since April, with a reserve held of around $36 million ready for the later and final push stages of the election campaign. Trump of course, declared himself a resident of the Sunshine State last year. Joe Biden is also pouring money in, albeit not on the same scale. $8 million spent on the airways with a reserve of $4million for later and final push stages. Another swing State where money is piling in is Arizona. Arizona has only voted for a Democratic President once since 1952 but it is looking to be a possibility this year with Biden squeaked into a tiny lead. The overriding story for American people though is still the pandemic, the President's inept handling of it, and subsequent economic fallout. There is a feeling that a Democratic win, for many, will breathe new life and hope. However, the incumbent President still pedals the view that if Biden wins it will be because the votes have

---

[41] New York Times. On Politics.

been tampered with.[42]

There is no factual basis for this argument, as indicated by evidence from those States who have expanded access to voting by mail amid the pandemic. Polling shows that a majority of the country supports universal access to mail-in voting, but if the White House succeeds in limiting access to mail-in ballots it could prevent millions of people in remote areas from voting full stop. Trump has voted by mail himself many times. [43]

Former President Barack Obama, off camera and at lucrative fundraisers, has been laying into Mr Trump. Following by credit of Shane Goldmacher and Glenn Thrush NYT. He highlights the numerous accusations of sexual assault levelled at The President. He also warns of the President's tendency to lean "nativist, sexist and racist" fears according to call records of Obama, donors, and others who have been party to calls. It seems that Obama's endorsement is bringing in the dollars with digital events over the last month have seen $24 million come in. Obama also levelled a swipe at Trump's interest in the preservation of confederate statues and monuments, saying it looks as if that is his number one priority right now. As the month closes, the death of Herman Cain, former CEO and Presidential Candidate, is announced. He was 74 and contracted the killer Covid-19 disease while attending the Trump rally in Tulsa in June. Credit NYT, Aimee Ortizo and Katharine Q Seelye.

In the United States of America, as of 31st July, there are: 4.59 million confirmed cases of Coronavirus and 155,000 deaths.

Globally; 17.3 million cases recorded and 674,000 deaths. [44]

---

[42] New York Times, On Politics.
[43] New York Times, On Politics.
[44] Multimedia sources.

DB 1st to 8th August

- John Lewis will lie in state in the Capitol Rotunda. One of the highest American honours, followed by a viewing for the public outside. As the Capitol is closed during the pandemic, the coffin will lie just a few hours then Monday and Tuesday outside to allow the public to pass at a suitable social distance.
- President Trump has cancelled the convention planned for Florida as the spreading virus makes an event of this scale untenable. Instead, he will schedule a much smaller meeting of Republican delegates in August in Charlotte.
- Last week the Democrats announced the downsize of their convention due in August from around 50,000 to maybe 300 attending. Tele-rallies and smaller events all round possibly.
- The Senate has adjourned for August, but talks continue to resolve the next stage of Coronavirus relief as the previous arrangement has ended. With Senators now back in home States, a meeting took place on Capitol Hill between Speaker Nancy Pelosi, Majority Leader Mitch McConnell, Mark Meadows, and White House Chief of Staff and Treasury Secretary Steve Mnuchin. Credit: NYT.
- The Democratic National Convention announces its cancellation due to the ongoing and, in some States, worsening pandemic. Nobody wants to or should travel, and Joe Biden will accept his presidential nomination from Delaware.
- In another U-turn, President Trump gives the go ahead for Microsoft to acquire the Chinese-owned video platform TikTok. The video app is due to close down September 15th unless someone buys it. Trump thought previously that it would be a threat to American intelligence due to cyber-attacks.
- Britain views the possibility of a Joe Biden win cautiously it is thought. Britain has long since courted relations with the American President and been engaging in post-Brexit trade

talks while trying to distance herself from Trump's errors. However, Joe Biden is opposed to Brexit, favours Ireland, and not much interested in trade talks with the UK government. Another Brexit problem for the UK.

- On Tuesday 4th August, a massive explosion at a storage facility of explosives in Lebanon killed close to 100 and injured 4,000 with the death toll expected to rise. The blast was felt for miles, even more than 100 miles away, hospitals were overwhelmed, and conspiracy theories abound. Initial reports are of an accident; the explosion's source being 2,750 tonnes of ammonium nitrate used in fertilizers and bombs kept there for six years. Neglect has cost hundreds of lives and devastation to thousands. It is reported on Thursday that the blast killed 135 and as many as 300,000 people are displaced from their homes. Authorities and hospitals are still overwhelmed while emergency services search for survivors. Lebanese officials said the dangerous cargo which exploded after six years in storage was destined for Mozambique but arrived on a Russian cargo ship and deemed unseaworthy and was impounded for failure to pay appropriate fees. In the following days thousands take to the street in protests against the government while the rescue continues amid a rising death toll. (Credit BBC News)

- Melbourne enforces strict lockdown measures and a 8 p.m. until 5 a.m. curfew to deal with a surge in Coronavirus cases. It is found that one in four who test positive and told to self-isolate are not doing so and authorities vow even tougher measures for six weeks. There are still around 500 new cases every day.

- Spain, Germany, France, Belgium, and Britain see spikes in cases and lockdown measures re-introduced while more countries are added to the list of needing to quarantine for 14 days if you travel to Britain.

- Britain imposes stricter local lockdowns where cases spike. This week Aberdeen has seen over 100 new cases spike from three bars in the city and eight players from Aberdeen Football Club involved. They broke rules and have been disciplined while pubs and restaurants close, no indoor visiting, and five-mile travel restrictions imposed for seven days. (Credit BBC News)

- In Britain, the Chancellor Rishi Sunak fends off questions as the country enters the deepest recession on records and the worst in Europe and any North American country. Britain's economy relies heavily on consumer spending, and it imposed a longer lockdown than most other countries and still easing off lightly. Also, by being slow to impose lockdown the virus spread rapidly, and the country suffered a huge death toll compared to other European hotspots. The fall in gross domestic product was twice as much as in America and Germany.

- New Zealand is back in lockdown after the first cluster of cases in months.

- Mexico reports 53,000 deaths and half a million cases.

- Israel reached an agreement with the United Arab Emirates on Thursday to establish "full normalisation of relations" and forego "declaring sovereignty" over occupied West Bank territory for now to improve ties with the rest of the Arab world. In the surprise announcement from the White House, President Trump said he had brokered a deal for Israel and UAE to cooperate on tourism security and other areas and moving towards direct flights between the countries to set up reciprocal embassies. The move is hailed as "historic" by both sides with Israel President Benjamin Netanyahu retweeting President Trump's announcement of the agreement. If successful the UAE will become the third country to establish relations with Israel after Jordan and Egypt.

- Britain sees the furlough scheme change where employers must now make a contribution to wages and National Insurance stamps. Some employers cannot afford to do that, and many workers are already being made redundant. More are expected when the scheme ends completely in October.

❏ The UK government looks to a "head of pandemic preparedness" to review the government's actions and to learn lessons from the Coronavirus crisis.

Once again, the daily brief feels too long and overwhelming, but I think it is all needed to show just what is happening at home, in the US, and around the world. There have of course been pandemics and wars before, bringing death and destruction, but the communication now is such that we hear about everything instantly. We also have better knowledge, science, and resources than ever before and yet being reactive rather than the proactive still seems to be how we are propelled through each day, wherever we are. Progress is there though, on many levels, so we must all keep going.[45]

---

[45] Sally Foster.

CHAPTER 25

Changing Gear En Route To The White House

According to Opensecrets.org campaign funds look like this:

Donald Trump, incumbent. Candidate committee money: $342,808,367.

Outside money:

$72,816,660.

Joe Biden, former Vice President.

Candidate Committee money:

$273,717,273.

Outside money:

$136,468,241.

Total funds raised by the active candidates $2,767 million dollars.

We are still waiting for the Vice President announcement with Karen Bass, Representative of California, and former Security Advisor Susan Rice joining the list of possibilities. All three are black. [46]Credit; Anna Moneymaker, Jonathan Martin and Alexander Burns, Katie Glueck. NYT political writers. Now, on the 5th of August, we are looking at a possible two-week delay in naming the Vice-President. The ladies in the running are beginning to be pitted

---

[46] Anna Moneymaker, Jonathan Martin, Alexander Burns, Katie Gluek,: New York Times political writers.

against each other while the President is using the opportunity to rake up mud on the potential rivals and use it against them. Still looking like a female, black most likely, but Elizabeth Warren remains a strong contender, along with Kamala Harris.[47]

While Trump continues to rail against mail-in ballots, he does, however, support it in Florida (where he is registered) because he says "it is a very well-run State," and attributes this to of course a "great Republican Governor." He is encouraging all to opt for a mail ballot in November. With both Republican and Democratic conventions now cancelled and moving to almost entirely virtual, this year has seriously challenged the traditions of American politics. Arguments continue between both sides on how to proceed with the next stage of the virus-relief initiative. By Saturday 8th August however, Congress discussions between Republicans and Democrats failed and President Trump signed four executive orders to address the issue directly. While the orders cover some assistance for people who rent properties and eases some student loans, it is not going to deliver cash to struggling Americans. His own aides also concede the order will not help small businesses, State, and local governments or low- and middle-income workers. All this as the United States Coronavirus cases pass five million. President Trump's want of criticizing Joe Biden goes on with the President saying Joe Biden is not a "man of God." Joe Biden hits back, highlighting how his Catholic Faith has helped him through many tough times.[48] (Credit NYT)

DB 9th to 16th August

❏   As Congress fails to agree on the next stage of virus relief, the President signs executive orders which are promptly deemed

---

[47] Washington Post, Annie Linsky.
[48] New York Times.

"unworkable, weak, and narrow" by Joint Democratic leaders. Nancy Pelosi calls the move "unconstitutional."

- The deadline for VP announcement draws ever closer as Biden folds down his selection committee and we await his decision.
- Meanwhile, rumours fly around that Kristi Noem is seeking the Republican VP ticket even although Trump has not indicated replacing Mike Pence.
- Later, on Tuesday 11th August, Joe Biden finally announces his running mate; Vice President is Senator Kamala Harris. She is 55 years old, of Indian/Jamaican parents and the first person of Indian descent to be on the ticket and only the fourth lady to be on a Presidential ticket. She is known to be a pragmatic moderate.
- Anger grows in Beirut and violent clashes on the streets. France President Macron visits and rallies the United Nations and over 30 countries to join forces and put together a package of aid and assistance. By the next day, the Government has resigned in Beirut. The devastation caused by the blast will take years to recover from.
- On 11th August in Scotland schools reopen. Some parents may hold back their children, and all are worried. The First Minister may need to pull back on pubs and restaurants as she wants to prioritise getting the young back to school after being off for five months. In London, Boris Johnson visits schools and pushes for full reopening but may follow Scotland's idea of pulling back pubs and restaurants.
- The cluster of cases of Coronavirus grows in Aberdeen after Premier League football team Aberdeen broke rules and players tested positive.
- A Celtic player also broke rules by flying to Spain and back, played a match, and did not quarantine for 14 days. The First Minister announces her anger and threatens to close down Premier League football if further breaches.

❏ Russia has approved a Coronavirus vaccine and puts into use. However, many are concerned it has been rushed and not proven, nor side effects known. Putin said one of his daughters has had the vaccine.

CHAPTER 26

Kamala Harris, Vice President

Finally, on 11th August 2020, just days before the Democratic Convention, Joe Biden announces his Vice President. Senator Kamala Harris, age 55 and of Indian/Jamaican parents, becomes only the fourth lady on the Presidential ticket and the first black lady ever. The Senator for California since 2017 previously ran for President but supported Biden once she dropped out, having been critical of him in the earlier Primaries. She supports police reform, proposed middle-class tax cuts, and pushed a Senate bill to make lynching a federal crime. Often electric in debate but has hit the occasional bump in debates and not articulated her point well. As a black lady in politics, she is thought to appeal to moderates and liberals. She advocates strongly for racial justice legislation, particularly in the aftermath of the George Floyd killing. Choosing Harris indicates Biden could well see her as the party leader in four- or eight-years' time.[49]

Following the announcement, Barack Obama and Hillary Clinton shower praise on the choice. So did many who had battled for the position. Top Republicans are not so impressed with the decision, calling her "nasty" and falsely labelling her "just about the most liberal person in the Senate." Vice President Mike Pence said, "the Democratic party have been overtaken by the radical left." [50]

As the day passes it appears the choice is not popular among leading Republicans and the negative ads begin. Rona McDaniel,

---

[49] New York Times by Alexander Burns, 2020 election reporter.
[50] New York Times.

Chairwoman of the Republican National Committee, said, "Kamala Harris' extreme positions show that left wing mob is controlling Biden's candidacy, just like they would control him as President." She also claimed, "these radical policies might be popular among liberals, but are well outside mainstream for most Americans." Five hours later the party puts out tweets criticizing Harris as not liberal enough. "Liberals revolt against Biden, Harris ticket." From the Trump side, she is viewed as a "radical liberal" and Fox News Tucker Carlson said she is "the single most transactional human being in America." A tough-on-crime cop and a left-wing Marxist. Trying to appease liberals while stoking war by disappointing progressive Democrats. Republicans view neither Harris or Biden as liberals but as vehicles to push a radical left-wing agenda. calling her "phony" and him "slow."

Kamala Harris spoke of her friendship with Beau Biden, Joe Biden's Son. Beau died in 2015 and during their friendship she knew that much of his inspiration and character developed from the guiding hand and closeness to his father. In less gentle terms the former California Attorney General spoke of the case against Pence and Trump. In an almost prosecutorial manner she placed the failures and crisis wrought by Coronavirus firmly at the President's administration door. Credit NYT/Nick Corasaniti. She went on to offer the Biden-Harris positive message and outlining the way forward. She spoke of a mandate showing that the past few years are not who America is and offering hope for who they (Democrats) aspire to be. [51]

In Biden's opening remarks at their first joint event, he spoke of the historic moment of having the first black female on the Presidential ticket. Of how little girls, black girls all over America woke up and instead of feeling as they often do, overlooked and undervalued, could for the first time see themselves as the stuff of Presidential candidacy. Credit Jennifer Medina/Evan Nicole Brown. The President and his campaign seemed to struggle to

---

[51] Katie Glueck, Thomas Kaplin in Delaware.

form cohesive retorts. Biden and Harris' first appearance together where they spoke as above was in Wilmington, Del.

Tom Perez, Chairman of the Democratic National Committee, has the headache of planning and delivering the first ever virtual convention which kicks off next week. The early planning, as it became apparent through the pandemic, showed that campaigning virtually is very much the way of the convention. Zoom is the way forward. People presenting from their own living rooms, but also in communities, in factories, first responders, and arguably with events coming in from all over America, possibly reaching more Americans than ever before on virtual platforms rather than an in-person convention. The core message will be "Build Back Better." Excitement is growing. [52]

During the Wilmington event, Joe Biden called for Americans to wear masks in public places for at least three months to help slow the spread of the virus which continues to wreak havoc across the country. Kamala Harris questioned Trump's push to find and develop a vaccine that would be safe. Trump questioned Harris' right to the candidacy, saying that as her parents were immigrants she did not meet the required terms, even though she was born in California. He did the same thing with Barack Obama. In customary form he mused that he assumed the Democrats had checked it out first, but he cast doubt, nevertheless. He also said he plans to deliver his Republican National Convention speech from the White House lawn. Questions abound over the legality of this in using a federal property for a campaign event. Further, Trump once again opposed more funding for the postal service in regard to mail-in voting only to change his mind again almost immediately. [53]

Since announcing Kamala Harris as VP, the Biden campaign has raised around $50 million. Money is pouring in from all over America. Polls continue to show Biden leading consistently across

---

[52] New York Times, Lisa Lerer.
[53] New York Times: Maggie Astor.

the last few months against the President. The Biden campaign spent big on TV ads this week at $14.6 million against Trump's $7million. On Facebook Biden spent $6,500 against Trump $1.2 million. [54]

DB 17th to 24th August

- ❏ A worsening situation in Belarus sees tens of thousands of people gather in Minsk for the biggest protest yet against President Alekzandr Lukashenko. Belarus is a former Soviet Republican which has been led by Lukashenko since 1994. He appealed for help from President Putin as rallies have been violent and so far dealt with by security forces, however, President Putin offered no confirmation of support.

- ❏ A salmon crisis in Russia makes headlines. A once plentiful supply has been victim of authorities allowing enterprises to string large nets across waters where wild fishing in the far east of Russia once gave plentiful supply. But now, amid poverty in the city of Khabarovsk on the Amur River, it brings more condemnation on President Putin who seems not to care for their plight.

- ❏ The trouble in Belarus continues as the once mighty dictator Alekzandr Lukashenko is weakened even as protesters are treated violently by his authorities. Europe's last dictator sees his power after 26 years slipping away as anger keeps growing among the people.

- ❏ In the UK following the release of exam results in England, Wales, and Northern Ireland, a week behind the Scottish school exams, all four devolved governments have now had to reverse and review decisions which saw an algorithm calculate grades. Many students had grades reduced and missed out on

---

[54] New York Times: Annie Karnie, Astead W Herndon.

University as a result. The outcry from all schools and governing bodies, students, parents, and teachers saw results changed where finally the grades predicted by the teachers were accepted. Universities review the places given and try to accommodate as many students as possible. Sadly, across all four nations some have missed out.

- In Belarus, the discontent goes on where the people are protesting at the re-election of the defiant President Alekzandr Lukashenko. The election is thought to have been corrupt by many but Lukashenko vows to go on regardless.
- In the UK, as schools and colleges return in Scotland, clusters of Coronavirus spring up although most are thought to have come from house parties among the youth before returning to the classroom. However, Scotland's infection rate remains low in comparison to England's.
- A new potential buyer for TikTok, the Chinese-owned video app, enters the arena. Oracle, better known for business software than social networking, expresses interest.
- A new US intelligence report says that top officials in Beijing were in the dark over Coronavirus in early January. It concludes that local officials in Wuhan and Hubei province had tried to hide information from central leadership.
- Britain announces an expansion to the testing process where a random sample of the population is tested, regardless of symptoms.
- The EU rejects the results of the election in Belarus. Not much will change as they do not wish to engage in conflict with Belarus and sanctions are already in place against Belarus and Russia.
- Trump's former advisor Steve Bannon is arrested and charged with fraud on Thursday (20th). He is charged with fraud. In a scheme tied to raising money to build the wall on the Mexican border, he and three others are charged with conspiring to

cheat thousands of donors and prosecutors said money was syphoned off and Bannon kept $1million for his personal expenses. The WE Build the Wall fund raised $25million from donors. Trump immediately distanced himself, saying he has not spoken with him for a long time.

- The Russian-produced Covid-19 vaccine (named Sputnik V) is called into question by many. Russian officials find themselves on the defensive and only 24 percent of Russian doctors say they would give the vaccine to patients.

- Russia's best-known critic of Vladimir Putin, Aleksei Nalvany, is reported to be in "serious but stable" condition in a Siberian hospital. It is suspected he was poisoned. Angela Merkel of Germany and Emmanuel Macron of France have offered assistance and or asylum to Nalvany. Mr Nalvany took so ill on a flight to Moscow the plane made an emergency landing. He had drunk tea at the airport before the flight which is thought to be how he may have been poisoned. The Kremlin posts out various deflections, saying he could have taken something himself, such as antidepressants or had been drinking heavily the night before, or was victim of a botched medical procedure in the West!

- President Trump voices once again his view that mail-in voting for the election in November will lead to corrupt or distorted results and is open to tampering.

- The Democrats National Convention kicks off on entirely virtual platforms this year, streaming live each evening 6 p.m. until 8 p.m. Pacific time with both the Obamas and Clintons due to speak.

- Over the weekend it was announced that President Trump's younger brother, Robert Trump, passed away after an illness. The President had visited him in hospital on Friday 14th August. They were close and he was a huge support to the President and Republican party.

- Kamala Harris, who has been quite vocal about her life as a black woman, acknowledges the influences also of her Indian mother and Indian grandparents.
- The first virtual Democratic National Conference begins with Michelle Obama and Bernie Sanders both concluding the first speeches and Eva Longoria as host. Mrs Obama was inspiring and Bernie Sanders threw his support wholeheartedly behind Joe Biden in an effort to rally all his supporters to vote Biden come November to have a chance of ousting Trump.
- In the DNC Joe Biden is formally nominated for President and Kamala Harris accepts the nomination for Vice President. Former President Barack Obama spoke on Wednesday, weighing in on the attack of Mr Trump, saying, "the Trump administration would tear down our democracy if that's what it would take to win."
- Florida becomes the fifth US State to see the death toll from Coronavirus reach over 10,000 people, according to a New York Times database.
- The US has poured billions of dollars into "Operation Warp Speed" to develop a vaccine but China and Russia, who have fast-tracked their way to questionable vaccines, has caused Trump to question, without evidence, the US Food and Drug Administration, accusing them of dragging their feet.
- In data compiled by The New York Times, the global death toll passes 800,000.

CHAPTER 27

Democratic National Convention – Virtual History

For the first time ever, the convention will be entirely virtual. So, as it kicks off today, just as polls show that Joe Biden's lead could be falling, what is happening at the event which will be live streaming on various platforms and therefore viewed possibly by more people than ever before?

Top speakers of the night include Michelle Obama, Bernie Sanders, and former Ohio Governor Josh Kasich. The event concludes on Thursday with Joe Biden accepting the formal nomination and delivering his keynote speech.[55]

This big virtual experiment is likely to be the Democrats best chance at reaching out to voters. The party has struggled to get airtime so far due to Trump's endless headlining tweets, the Coronavirus pandemic, and all the news coming from Black Lives Matter and social injustices. A busy year. How this week works may not change the outcome of the election, but it will show what the party stands for in this Trump era and what the hopes and dreams are for a better future. Daily headline reporting from here along with the NYT Politics team with chat, live briefing, and analysis. Looking firstly at UNITY. A diverse roster of speakers could prove a challenge in showing a cohesive future agenda. Perhaps they need to show a clear plan even with differences in

---

[55] CNN Eric Bradner, Gregory Krieg.

their own party on the way forward. MR NOVEMBER. Joe Biden has been in politics for around 50 years. His performance so far and in the primaries are a bit questionable, however. His keynote speech on Thursday night is the most important of this 50-year career. He needs to deliver. Americans need to be convinced of a clear message. COME TOGETHER. Most speakers have around a two-minute slot to speak but Joe Biden has eight minutes. Economic recovery, health care, and foreign policy are a source of division in the Democratic party even now. Sanders so far has backed Biden but with his own two-minute slot, will he push more of his own agenda or keep backing Joe Biden? [56]

As I live in Scotland I will not be watching a live stream as in the UK that will be 2 a.m. until 4 p.m. As with most of this study, I will be relying on the daily brief and On Politics from the New York Times. *However, I will be watching on Amazon Prime Video and any other platform available to me, drawing some of my own conclusions.* The Times *is live streaming, YouTube, Facebook, Twitter, and Twitch following. ABC, CBS, NBC, and Fox News alongside a host of other channels, stations, and outlets in media. You can watch on a PS4, or PSVR through the Littlestar app. I could ask "Alexa" to "play the Democratic National Convention." Exciting times in America while the relentless difficulties of the pandemic impact on us all and, in the UK, Brexit talks are rarely mentioned even though the deadline is looming.* [57]

Day 1

Michelle Obama Speech

The former first lady spoke eloquently and was inspiring,

---

[56] New York Times; Lisa Lerer.
[57] Sally Foster.

delivering a searing indictment of the sitting President. Saying that he is "in over his head," "cannot meet this moment," and "he simply cannot be who we need him to be for us." Michelle Obama delivers confidence in a way that will reach out to those voters crucial to the Biden success, such as swing district suburban women and sporadic voters. She called for political leaders to "reflect our truth" and within minutes women's activists' groups were tweeting affirmation. Her message was clear. Trump can't do the job. If he is re-elected, things will get worse and get worse quickly. "Vote for Biden, our lives depend on it," her rallying message.

Bernie Sanders Speech

Bernie Sanders was criticized in 2016 for not fully endorsing Hillary Clinton and many mused that he may even now push his own agenda rather than rally support for Joe Biden. However, he certainly left no room for doubt in his support for Biden, regardless of policy issue differences, calling for all his supporters to vote for Biden. He proclaimed a Biden administration would fight to raise the minimum wage to $15 per hour, create 12 weeks of paid family leave, fund universal pre-kindergarten, and transition the country to clean electricity over 15 years. He did, however, concede slightly on the healthcare, saying that although he and Biden differ slightly on this policy he believes Biden will deliver on a plan that will expand healthcare and cut the cost of prescription drugs while in addition lowering the eligibility age from 65 to 60 for Medicare. In closing the man who ushered in a new era of progressive power for the Democratic party said, "my friends, the cost of failure is just too great to imagine." Another speech worthy of a mention came from Kristen Urquisa, the Arizona student who wrote an impassioned obituary for her father, citing two causes of death being the Coronavirus and the ineptitude of government officials. She said of her father, "his only pre-existing condition was Trump, and for that he paid with his life." Already her words are being spliced into an ad running in Arizona and Nevada for Nuestro PAC who are a group aiming to mobilise Latino voters. [58]

Day 2

Jill Biden steps up tonight to speak, declaring "the heart of this nation still beats with kindness and courage … That's the soul of America Joe Biden is fighting for now."

In 2019 Democrats debated finer details of key issues around student debt, fossil fuels, and healthcare. 2020 and squabbles are washed away or at least parked until inauguration day. The second night of the convention drew focus on a single promise of a return to normal life while dealing with the impacts of devastation from the pandemic and social unrest. Speakers from across the country represented a fine picture of multiracial democracy with Dr Biden hailing her husband as a leader with all the right qualities for a President. National security officials spoke of restoring the country's place on the world stage and the evening is dominated by fine testimonials to Joe Biden's character. In counterbalance, though, personal attacks on Trump came to the fore with former Secretary of State, John Kerry, saying, "He won't defend our country. He doesn't know how to defend our troops. The only person he's interested in defending is himself." Former President Bill Clinton added weight, saying, "If you want a President who defines the job as spending hours a day on watching TV and zapping people on social media, he's your man." Tonight's clear message, beating Trump is everything.

Some notable Republicans again voiced support on the night for Joe Biden. Colin Powell, former Secretary of State under George W Bush and who made the case for the Iraq war and was

---

[58] New York Times; Lisa Lerer, Nick Corasaniti.

subsequently renounced by many in the Democratic party, was embraced by the very same party tonight.

With 17 different speakers, there was lots of information to take in but the lengthy addresses came from Mr Clinton, Mr Kerry, Mr Powell, and Dr Biden. And Democrats formally nominated Joseph R Biden Jr for the Presidency. [59]

Denied a chance to gather in person in Milwaukee due to the pandemic, activists and dignitaries cast their votes for the nomination from across all 50 states, the American territories, and the district of Columbia. Joe Biden appeared with his wife in a Delaware school while his grandchildren burst in with balloons and streamers quoting "no malarkey." Joe Biden's favourite phrase, or at least one of them. He quipped back "see you all on Thursday" which is when he will formally accept the nomination. Hosted by actress Tracee Ellis Ross, the evening offered music and entertainment alongside themes of national security, presidential continuity, and offerings from past and future leaders of the party.

Day 3

Day three continues with the same format for the convention but the focus clearly on the backbone of the Democratic party being Black voters, Latino voters, and women. In short those who have injected the party with new energy around injustices. Keynote speaker Kamala Harris, having accepted the nomination for Vice President, said, "Let's be clear – there is no vaccine for racism." She went on to name victims of police violence including George Floyd. Ms Harris, the first black woman and the first woman of Indian descent to be on the presidential ticket, also noted the 100th anniversary of the adoption of the 19th amendment and of women's suffrage.

---

[59] New York Times, On Politics; Lisa Lerer, Nick Corasaniti.

In a second major speech of the evening, former President Barack Obama was forthright in his blistering attack on President Trump. He went on to encourage those young people who took to the streets to protest against injustices, telling them "in so many ways you are this country's dreams fulfilled." In a night where most speakers were women, Harris and Obama were preceded by speeches from Hillary Clinton, Senator Elizabeth Warren, and speaker Nancy Pelosi. Critics, however, noted a lack of Latino speakers. With just one more evening event to go, excitement mounts in preparation for Joe Biden to deliver his keynote speech on Thursday, accepting formally the nomination and inspiring his party and voters to join together and VOTE.

Day 4

Joe Biden seized the moment to make this count! The unconventional convention offered a greater opportunity perhaps than in all previous conventions for him to deliver a different kind of speech. A direct-to-camera speech making it more intimate, more personal than in a normal manner in a big venue. Where Trump had urged voters on Thursday to vote for him to stop Biden's mayhem coming to town, Joe Biden cast himself as the way out of this national crisis. "I will draw on the best of us, not the worst." He said. "I will be an ally of the light, not the darkness." Biden can often be an uneven speaker but tonight, none of that apparent. In fact, one of the best speeches in his 50-year political career. Putting to rest the rumours sent out by Trump and supporters that Biden is not up to the task, and supposedly they say mentally and physically unfit for the job. Without ever saying Trump's name, Joe Biden launched a simmering criticism of the incumbent President. in particular focusing on the economic crisis at Trump's hands which is one of the Republican campaign's key issues. "While I will be a Democratic candidate I will be an American President. That's the job, to represent all of us." He went on to say that on the ballot is "character, compassion, decency, science, and democracy". "Who we are, what we stand for, and who we want to be as a Nation."

The week may have been light on policy and heavy on character and indeed not much policy came about in Biden's speech, but he did outline the four crisis areas which he sees as key. The pandemic, the economy, racial injustice, and climate change. But first the campaign has to happen and the election then the work, he promises, can begin. The emerging plan seems to be to keep focus on the President's failings and hail ever more loudly Joe Biden's strengths. For decades Joe Biden has talked his way through campaigns and conventions. Four years ago, he mourned his son Beau in front of sympathetic friends and allies. This year, he spoke almost entirely alone, in a hall with just around 30 journalists, masked and socially distanced. After his speech he stood outside wearing a mask and watching fireworks over a drive-in viewing in his home state of Delaware. Not a typical end of convention shot but a powerful image of where the country is at this moment in time. [60]

Numbers

To quickly recap the numbers over the week, the Biden campaign raised 70 million dollars during the four-day convention.

21.8 million people tuned in for Biden's keynote speech on Thursday, slightly more than the 21 million who watched former President Obama and Senator Kamala Harris on Wednesday.

A new Gallup poll puts Trump's approval rating at 42 percent. 48 percent approval on handling the economy which is the focus so far of the Trump campaign. Three separate polls still have Biden on average eight points ahead of Trump.

---

[60] New York Times. New York Times; Lisa Lerer, Astead Herndon, Annie Karnie.

Even by Republicans the virtual DNC was hailed a success. Trump has been slow to embrace the concept of a virtual Convention and is still looking to dominate all four days himself. Perhaps he needs to learn quickly but probably too late to put on the same professional display. Either way he needs to find a way to appeal to a broader base than the traditional Republican voters.[61]

DB 25th to 31st August

- ❑ A team at the University of Hong Kong found the first case of reinfection of Coronavirus four months after the first infection. It looks like a different strain which was circulating in Europe where the patient had travelled to Spain via Britain in July and August.
- ❑ Usain Bolt, eight-time Olympic champion, has tested positive for Coronavirus and is in self-isolation.
- ❑ Aleksei Navalny, the Russian critic of Putin who was flown to Germany for treatment, is in a stable condition. Doctors suggest he was poisoned, and fingers are pointed at Putin. Russian authorities dismiss it.
- ❑ In the UK, the government's "eat out to help out" scheme which allows diners 50% off their bill on eat-in food and drink is hugely successful. The government pays the 50% to the restaurant. The scheme runs Monday to Wednesday and ends on 31st August.
- ❑ Two more cases of re-infection were reported in Europe.
- ❑ In March last year, Brenton Rarrant murdered 55 Muslims during Friday prayers in a Christchurch mosque. On 26th August he was sentenced to life in prison with no opportunity for parole. The country's most severe sentence.

---

[61] New York Times, On Politics.

- In Belarus, President Alekzandr Lukashenko called on President Putin for help. He duly ordered a special force of officers to be created to deal with the protestors if the situation gets out of control. For more than two weeks protestors have called for Lukashenko to step down amid the row over a corrupt election which many EU leaders agreed was compromised.

- For the third Sunday in a row, and as protests enter the fourth week, thousands of protesters march in Belarus, calling for the resignation of Lukashenko. Although relatively peaceful on this occasion, around 100 protestors were detained by security forces.

- Millions of pupils have returned to school in Scotland. Full safety measures are in place and school pupils in senior school must now also wear face coverings in public areas between classes and on school transport. A few schools have had positive cases of the virus with pupils self-isolating, but most are thought to have been contracted before return to school after summer break due to house/indoor gatherings.

- The Republican Democratic Convention rolls onto day two. Trump intends to speak every day.

- In Florida, a judge struck down Gov. Ron DeSantis' order requiring public schools to open for in-person classes. Judge Charles W. Dodson of Leon County Circuit Court wrote that the order which threatened to withhold funds from school districts that did not give the option of returning in person violated the State constitution because it "arbitrarily disregards safety."

- On the second evening of the RNC, Melania Trump takes to the stage. Or at least, The Rose Garden of the White House. In contrast to the first evening when speeches focussed on a bleak future for America under a Biden administration, Melania spoke of "kindness and compassion, strength and determination."

- Speaking from a Jerusalem rooftop, Mike Pompei broke from tradition being the first sitting secretary of state for at least 75 years to address a national party conference. But on Tuesday, the House foreign affairs subcommittee investigated as the chairman said the speech could violate the Hatch Act which is a Depression-era law which bans federal employees from engaging in political activities while in post.

- In Wisconsin riots rage on after the police shooting of a black man, Jacob Blake He is now paralysed. Now an Illinois teenager, Kyle Rittenhouse, aged 17, has been charged with first-degree intentional homicide after a shooting in the unrest left two people dead and one injured. Trump vows to send in more National Guard numbers to squash the unrest.

- On day four of the RNC President Trump accepted the party nomination to run again for President. He framed the election as a crossroads for America in the usual manner of condemning Biden while failing to set out much of a plan for his promise to "make America great again."

- A man was shot dead in Portland, Oregon, after a large group of Trump supporters drove a caravan into the city where demonstrators are gathering nightly to protest against police violence and racism. Trump reinforces his wish to bring in the National Guard to deal with such troubles.

CHAPTER 28

The Republican National Convention, Unconventionally!

In his acceptance speech of 2016, and in front of a divided Republican party, Donald Trump declared that he alone would fix it. Almost four years in it seems the party is no longer so divided with eight out of ten saying they remain loyal to the President, and most Republicans it seems intend to vote for him. He remains broadly unpopular across America with his handling of the pandemic and the beleaguered economy the top issues which see him trailing Joe Biden across most polls by an average of eight points. Yet, his old mantra "I alone can fix it" is rolled out again on day one in 2020! Having been officially nominated in Charlotte on day one, he gave a speech and plans as we know to speak each night in the televised broadcasts of the convention where normally just one keynote speech is the routine. William Kristol, a Republican critic of Trump, tweeted, "it's no longer the Republican party, it's a Trump cult." He went on to release a list of 27 Republican former members of Congress who endorse Joe Biden.

Mike Pence also spoke after accepting his own nomination for Vice President during which he said that backing Mr Trump was tantamount to supporting key G.O.P policy positions. He spoke of key Republican issues that Trump stands for, including free market economics, secure borders, and opposition to abortion. Further speakers include Nikki Hailey, Trump's former UN ambassador, Representative Jim Jordan of Ohio, and Senator Tim

Scott of South Carolina, the only Black Republican in the Senate.

Nytimes.com will be online to offer analysis live. CNN, MSNBC, and PBS will show the full two-hour broadcast, but other major TV networks will only air the second half. Fox News may air some of the first half.[62]

While all this positive vibe is being projected, the reality is actually grim. Nearly 1,000 Americans are dying daily from Covid-19. Unemployment claims back up to 1.1 million in a week. On Sunday, Jacob Blake, a black man in Wisconsin, was shot in the back multiple times by the police and in front of his children. And the President's finances are being investigated by the New York attorney general. But come Monday night the speakers tried to encourage voters to forget the last six months and re-elect the president who once saw a booming economy. They tried to cast Trump as a compassionate leader, branding Joe Biden as left-wing and also hail the President's handling of the current crisis gripping the country as successful. A bit of a big ask in an empty auditorium perhaps. [63]

Day 2

Last week the Republicans said their convention would be more upbeat than the Democrats and promised hope for a bright future, and while it didn't start that way on Monday, Tuesday's message was "Land of Opportunity" and featured video packages and earnest speeches from small business owners and numerous Trump supporters without the National profile. However, any message offering "hope" was looking to a post-pandemic recovering country and the speakers largely ignored the pandemic and the ravages of it throughout America. Larry Kudlow, the President's top advisor, spoke of it in the past tense, hinting that

---

[62] New York Times; Giovanni Russonello.
[63] New York Times; Lisa Lerer, Nick Corasaniti.

the heartache and hardship was a lingering after effect rather than an actual in-the-moment scenario. Even in delivery of speeches the virus was ignored as Melania Trump was not wearing a mask and neither were the attendees in The Rose Garden and social distancing was also ignored. Not everyone had been tested for the virus prior to attending either. The only nod to the virus was an expression of sympathy from the First Lady in her speech which closed the evening as she expressed sympathy for those suffering and for the bereaved. It looks like the Trump campaign has not yet figured out how to deal with the pandemic and offer the promised hope while campaigning for re-election.[64]

In June, the Republican party said it would not write a 2020 platform and has instead carried over the 2016 version word for word, including more than three dozen outdated condemnations of the "current" President which, when the document was written, was Barack Obama. A party platform has little to do with candidate campaigns or would govern as President, it has for more than 100 years been a guide for the party's political beliefs. So effectively Republicans have said that party principles and priorities have not changed in the Trump term.[65]

On the question of racial injustices which the DNC addressed in their convention, the message from the Republicans is quite different although they do hope to attract the so-called "black vote" and other ethnic minorities. To this end Nikki Hayley said, "America is not a racist country" as she accused the Democrats of being unpatriotic in its condemnation of discrimination prevalent in America in their view. On the first night nobody mentioned Jacob Blake, a black man shot by police multiple times in the back by police in Wisconsin as he tried to break up a fight. Nor did anyone mention the racial wealth gap or impact of pollution on the black communities. In fact, Republicans in general portrayed the protestors as violent and extremists who would run amok under a

---

[64] New York Times; Lisa Lerer, Nick Corasaniti.
[65] Reid J Epstein.

Joe Biden administration. Moments after Nikki Hayley's speech, Donald Trump Jr continued on the same theme saying the Democrats are attacking the principles on which the nation is founded and accuses them of trying to cancel history and the nation's founders. He painted a grim picture of America with Biden in the White House and claimed that "911 calls will go to voicemail." The message that the Democrats prefer anarchy over order and a threat to safety define Trump's re-election campaign. Rife with undertones and no doubt much more to come this week, will it stick? Before the DNC, a NBC News/Wall Street Journal poll asked voters to name two top issues they consider when voting in November. 15 percent mentioned crime, but 51 percent mentioned the economy, 43 percent a united country, strong leadership 34 percent, healthcare 29 percent, and the Coronavirus 27 percent. In a range of polls most show on those issues people see Joe Biden more capable than Trump. [66]

Day 3

Finally, we see the Republicans lay out a strategy for the re-election of President Trump. Mike Pence, in his speech, finally acknowledged the issues facing the country and making a case for voters to support Trump. His speech addressed the major issues tearing through the American way of life from the pandemic to social injustices and for a party known for so far ignoring the seriousness of the situation it is something of a departure. The crowd once again chose not to wear masks, at least most of them didn't as he spoke at Fort McHenry National Monument in Baltimore. He also said the choice is not about being Republican or Democrat but about America being America. He spoke of how well the President handled the pandemic at the very beginning but

---

[66] New York Times; Lisa Lerer, Nick Corasaniti.

ignored his continued efforts to downplay the virus spreading still and the lack of a cohesive federal response. On the racial injustices he claimed the protesters are left-wing radicals. But when referring to recent shootings of protests and police officers he ignored the fact that the authorities have investigated suspects possible ties with vigilante or far-right extremist groups. There were of course the usual unfounded attacks on Joe Biden. Yet, he managed to address the protests, telling the crowd the American people did not have to choose between Black Americans and the police. He promised progress on a vaccine. And tried to re-cast the President as a "family man". He went on to affirm that the President has "kept his word" when in reality the last four years have shown that the President has not always kept his word and further, he frequently changes his mind. It is still not clear what the President's message is or what he would do to "make America great again." It is also not clear how he would address the issues he is accused of mismanaging so far, especially since the pandemic. On healthcare alone the President's administration is currently trying to dismantle the Affordable Care Act which could see 54 million Americans with pre-existing conditions missing out on health insurance coverage. Like all of us just now, the President's campaign wishes they were living and campaigning in different times. Since January when we first heard rumblings of a virus in China, little did anyone know what was to come and it is still changing lives. [67]

Day 4

On the final night President Trump will have his big chance to shine. He is expected to condemn the Democrats' extremism and Chinese aggression while also trying to appeal to voters in the centre around childcare and education. He will no doubt try to win

---

[67] New York Times; On politics.

back the suburban women who have turned away from him. Others due to speak on the closing evening are Ben Carso, secretary of housing and urban development, Rudolph W. Giuliani, former Mayor of New York and the President's private lawyer, and Senator Tom Cotton of Arkansas.

So, in 2016 Trump accepted the nomination at the RNC with a speech painting a dark vision of the nation under siege. He spoke of terrorism, the attacks on the police, and promised that on January 20th, 2017 safety would be restored. He said he could fix it. Ironic then perhaps that four years later President Trump is speaking about "anarchists, agitators, rioters, looters and flag-burners." But once again he declares he alone can "fix it." Elections historically have become more or less a referendum between the incumbent President and the policies and personality of the challenger. But in 2020 it seems more of a referendum on Trump's leadership. Joe Biden has kept a low profile and let Trump be the author of his own misfortune. The polls point at most Americans feeling like the President has mismanaged the pandemic which is still raging through the country. It is somehow bizarre that the President, the Commander-in-chief in the highest office in the land, feels himself "an outsider" and blames the political establishment for the troubles roaring through the country by way of protests and unrest. He has sent in law enforcements and yet still said "the problem could be fixed if they wanted it to be, just call … We have to wait for the call." Shouldn't he take charge or at the very least be a leader? The convention was more about decrying Biden than setting out policies or strategies or "the fix." Has his lack of plan, politics, and strategy left voters with choosing between an incumbent President with all his known faults and foibles and perceived failings and his very famous personality or an altogether more organised, and increasingly more popular choice of Joe Biden? As the race enters the final stages it will no doubt become closer while the Coronavirus, economy, social and racial injustices, and healthcare dominate both agendas.

On Friday, the day after the convention ended in Charlotte, Robert Trump's private funeral took place at the White House. [68]

Numbers

Global Covid-19 as of 31st August 2020:
25 million+ and 842,700 deaths.
Covid-19 in USA as of 31st August 2020:
6 million+ and 183k deaths.
Covid-19 in UK as of 31st August 2020:
334K + and 41,499 deaths.

Campaign Funds raised as of 31st August 2020:
Trump Candidate Committee Money – $414,585,720.
Outside Money – $90,212,572.
Biden Candidate Committee Money – $321,046,082.
Outside Money – $148,532,827.
Total funds raised by active candidates 2020 election campaign: $2,887.4 million.[69]

DB 1st to 8th September

- A second wave of Coronavirus sweeps across Spain with 54,000 cases in the last week, pushing infection rate to 114 per 100,000 people. Spain eased lockdown and opened up fairly quickly and now the virus is spreading faster there than in the US, the UK, Italy, and Germany.
- Australia recorded their highest daily death toll on Monday, all within the state of Victoria.

---

[68] New York Times; On Politics team including Lisa Lerer, Nick Corasaniti, Giovanni Russonello.
[69] Open Secrets.

❏ New Zealand reported 14 new cases on Tuesday. Five community cases linked to a cluster in the largest city of Auckland.

❏ Russian opposition leader Aleksei Navalny is still in a coma in a German hospital. It is thought he was poisoned. Putin denies any involvement. But Nalvany's organisation, the anti-corruption foundation, released a video on Monday of Nalvany denouncing pro-Kremlin politicians in Siberia.

❏ It is announced early on Wednesday by the German government that Navalny has been poisoned with Novichok as traces are found in his system. This has been used before in poisoning of other Russian dissidents.

❏ President Macron of France makes a second visit to Lebanon within a month and urges them to back an overhaul of government and measures to curb corruption while warning that if they don't they could be subject to sanctions on their personal wealth. Macron hopes the threat of sanctions will secure a commitment to economic and political measures previously discussed this year in looking at an International Monetary fund bail-out. Talks stalled earlier this year over multiple issues including the government's refusal to submit to a forensic audit of the central Bank.

❏ German chancellor Angela Merkel demands answers from Russia as doctors treating Aleksei Navalny in Germany confirm he was poisoned with Novichok, a deadly substance which can and has killed people.

❏ Chancellor Angela Merkel of Germany is under pressure to scrap the $11 billion deal with Russia for a gas pipeline amid the accusation from Russia that Aleksei Navalny "poisoned himself," "story is fake," or "the poisoning never happened at all." Even members of her own party have called for her to call off the programme, called Nord Stream 2.

- For the fourth Sunday in a row tens of thousands of protestors flood through the towns and cities of Belarus. The tide of protest against the re-election of President Lukashenko shows no sign of abating. President Putin of Russia, late last month, having been slow to offer support to Lukashenko, has now formed a reserve of security forces should they be needed in Belarus.
- As schools have returned and gyms and pools reopen in Scotland, the UK reports the highest daily toll of positive Coronavirus tests since May when in full lockdown with 2,988 reported for the four nations on Sunday. The majority are in England, where schools return today with 208 in Scotland, also the highest daily total, and 98 in Wales.
- On Brexit Boris Johnson has said that the UK could walk away from talks within weeks if agreement is not reached by October 15th and went on to say that a no-deal exit would be a good outcome for the UK.
- BBC News reports that the Russian opposition leader Aleksei Navalny is out of an induced coma in hospital and that his condition has improved.
- In a bizarre twist in Belarus, it is reported that Maria Kolesnikova, the last prominent protest leader in Belarus, has disappeared. Reports suggest she was grabbed by kidnappers in the centre of Minsk, bundled into a van and driven away.
- Spain becomes the first and so far only European country to exceed half a million Coronavirus cases with 525,549 reported.
- As some schools return to in-person classes in the US, cases in children and young people are rising faster than in the general public.
- After the shooting in Portland, Oregon, and further outbreaks of violent protests in Kenosha in Wisconsin, President Trump argues and tweets that the violence in Portland is driven by "agitators and anarchists."

- Trump further says the only way to stop the violence is through strength. He shared a video on Twitter of his supporters firing tear gas into protestors in Portland. Declared "the big backlash going on in Portland cannot be unexpected."
- As schools return in the US to in-person teaching, many parents keep their children home. They are rightly worried about their safety as the Coronavirus is spreading through children and students faster than before. If restrictions remain in place in bars, restaurants, etc., how can it be safe in school, they ask.
- Joe Biden hits out at the President as Trump insists he can keep the country safe. Biden, speaking in Pittsburgh yesterday (31st), insists that Trump is fanning the flames of unrest. Biden condemns those protests in Portland and Kenosha who have lit fires and been violent and destructive but went on to remind people that this situation is happening on Trump's watch and not his. He reminds people that Trump is failing to stop his supporters acting as "armed militia" and calls him weak.
- Trump does nothing over the weekend in a press conference to prove Biden wrong and fails to condemn his supporters using violence in clashes with protestors calling for racial justice. He refused to condemn his caravan of supporters driving through Portland firing paint bullets at protestors, saying paint is a "peaceful protest." He defended Kyle Rittenhouse, a 17-year-old who was arrested and charged after video footage showed him shooting three people, two of whom died, in Kenosha last week. He said, "he was trying to get away from them."
- Trump visits Kenosha on Tuesday as the governor warns him against it as well as leading Democrats. It is believed it will just provoke further unrest.
- In Pennsylvania, a poll by Monmouth University found that Biden's 13-point lead in July has shrunk to four points. Not great news in the swing State/battleground areas. However,

Fox News viewed Biden ahead in Arizona, North Carolina, and Wisconsin.

- Joe Biden visits Kenosha and the message is in stark contrast to Trump's visit this week. He spoke on the phone to Jacob Blake's family where Trump ignored them.
- Also, President Trump spoke at a rally in Pennsylvania last night where he mocked Biden for wearing a mask on the visit to Kenosha and went further by appearing to encourage people to vote twice! Once by mail and also in-person under the pretext of testing the integrity of the mail-in ballots. Voting twice is illegal so it is not clear what point Trump is making here.
- Nate Cohen, of *The Times*, notes that in national and critical battleground States Trump is trailing Biden.
- Wildfires raging through California State are thought to have been started by a "gender reveal party."

CHAPTER 29

Rolling into September as Biden Speaks Out Against Trump

President Trump's visit to Kenosha unsurprisingly upset many. They spoke of the police officer who shot Jacob Blake in the back seven times last week as being similar to a golfer who chokes on a putt. He was trying to make the point that an officer can have a clean exemplary record then under pressure make a mistake. He met with law enforcement officers in Kenosha as he visited burned-out business as he tried to bring attention to the destruction caused by the protestors and described their actions as "domestic terror." Trump did not meet with Blake's family who opted to attend a separate event on the block where Blake was shot. Jesse Jackson was also present in what became a community event. [70]

When Joe Biden visited Kenosha, he spoke with the family of Jacob Blake over the phone, he wore a mask and he of course spoke out against the lack of humanity shown by the President on his visit. While the President spoke at a rally in Pennsylvania, he predictably continued his attacks on Joe Biden, mocking him for wearing a mask and seemingly encouraging voters to vote twice, by mail and in person. Trailing in the polls it did not look like Trump put out much positive news or offered much hope and it is not clear what he was in fact trying to do with this speech.

---

[70] New York Times, Giovanni Russonello.

At the State Assembly in the California State Capitol, Buffy Wicks spoke with her new-born daughter swaddled in her arms which is perhaps an image reflective of where things are with the pandemic. Miss Wicks, a veteran of the Obama and Clinton campaigns, had arrived to vote on several crucial bills on the last day of the legislative session. Miss Wicks lives in Oakland which is an hour or so south-west of Sacramento and since being elected to the State Assembly in 2018 has mostly made it home for her elder daughter's bedtime but the juggling was on this occasion too much. As well as voting she stood in a mask with a baby swaddled in her arms and delivered her powerful speech on the legislative floor. The backstory here is that voting by proxy while on maternity leave did not seem to fit in the parameters and perhaps the validity of the vote could be questioned. Colleagues were asking her to attend as some crucial bills needed crucial votes. So, after discussing with her husband, colleagues, and the speaker, Miss Wicks decided to travel with the baby and vote. Not easy and to her credit. [71]

As this first weekend in September arrives the summary of the week post-convention is much like the weeks before. President Trump has focused on law enforcement while condemning rioters and protestors as anti-American. Mr Biden hit back while acknowledging right-wing vigilantes are a big part of the problem and that racism must be driven out of law enforcement in order to help heal the country. He also sought to turn the directive back to the pandemic and the President's failure to handle it and also his failures in other key areas like economy, social and racial injustices, to name but a few. As voters ask questions and decide where their vote goes, it still seems a long way from clear policy or planning from either party. [72]

The Biden camp announced they had raised $364.5 million in August and plan to spend $45 million on digital and TV ads this

---

[71] New York Times; Giovanni Russonello.
[72] New York Times; Giovanni Russonello

month. The Trump camp has not disclosed their funds raised in August. The polls did indicate that the expected narrowing of the gap had arrived but not as close as was expected and the race it seems is still to really start, with Trump trailing.

Kamala Harris and Mike Pence visit Wisconsin with very different agendas and messages. As the Democrats beef up campaigning, Kamala Harris meets with Jacob Blake's family. Blake, a 29-year-old black man who has been left paralysed after being shot seven times by police, is in constant pain in hospital. Kamala Harris wanted to show her support for the family. While in the Milwaukee area Harris also toured an International Brotherhood of Electrical workers training centre and met with Union members. It is Labor Day in the US. Mike Pence, on his visit, did not mention Blake by name but continued on the theme that rioters and looting is not free speech nor peaceful protest. Of course, it is not. He went on to criticize Biden for not dealing with Democratic Mayors who have allowed violent protests, looting, burning buildings etc. without really challenging or bringing into order. He said that Biden as President would lead to further unrest across America. [73]

DB 8th to 14th September

❏ In Belarus Maria Kolesnikova has reappeared in her country near the border with Ukraine. There, after passing through a checkpoint, she destroyed her own passport making it impossible for Ukraine to admit her. Ukraine's Minister for foreign affairs said the woman had been brave and had thwarted the attempt of the authorities in Belarus to forcibly expel her from the country. She remains on Belarus territory. The unrest has continued since an alleged corrupt election on August 9th, now one full month.

---

[73] New York Times, Giovanni Russonello.

- AstraZeneca has been forced to halt a vaccine trial as one person shows adverse reactions. The person was enrolled in phase ⅔ in Britain. It is still to be determined if the volunteer's illness is directly due to the vaccine. The British/Swedish company is following procedure to investigate fully before trials can re-commence.

- Brexit talks stalled again with Prime Minister Boris Johnson setting October 15th as deadline for decision on trade deals. After that it could well be a no-deal exit.

- A fire ripped through perhaps the world's largest refugee camp on the Greek Island of Lesbos. It is thought to have been started intentionally by a small group of camp residents. They were protesting at quarantine measures after 35 people tested positive for Covid-19. The pandemic has aggravated tensions between Islanders and the migrants. The government also tightened borders.

- In the UK on the 9th September, Boris Johnson announced new measures to control the spread of the virus as cases reach over 2,500 in a 24-hour period which includes telling people to meet up in social groups of no more than six people from two households inside or outside. On the 10th the First Minister of Scotland announced the same restrictions with some exemptions and exceptions.

- A new NHS test and protect app is launched in Scotland to help the track and trace method of protecting ourselves and others.

- EU issues an ultimatum to the UK over the proposed withdrawal deal changes. The UK has published a bill to rewrite parts of the previously agreed signed withdrawal agreement. The UK remains firm that Parliament is sovereign and can pass laws which breach the UK's International treaty obligations. The bill concerns the Internal Market Bill which addresses the Northern Ireland protocol (designed to prevent a hard border returning to Ireland) and gives UK ministers powers to modify or "disapply" rules relating to goods that will come into force from January 1ˢᵗ if the UK and EU are unable to strike a trade deal. The EU urges the UK to withdraw the bill by the end of the month or face legal consequences (BBC News).

- Corruption behind last month's Beirut explosion is outlined as it emerges that the lethal cocktail of explosives was reported to authorities by staff at the plant, but nothing was done even in spite of an order from a Judge. 190 people were killed and more than 6,000 injured.
- The global death toll reaches 900,000 from Coronavirus and has touched almost every country or territory in the world.
- Astra/Zeneca restart the vaccine trials.
- The 5ᵗʰ Sunday of protests in Belarus sees tens of thousands more people with many waving the banner of the former flag which Lukashenko banned when he came to power in 1994.
- Covid-19 cases continue to surge in Britain as all four Nations impose further restrictions for meeting with other households inside or outside and in any setting of pubs, bars, and restaurants while phase four easing of lockdown in Scotland is delayed. Furlough is due to end in October and many businesses cannot yet reopen so huge job losses are expected. The Chancellor is under pressure to extend the furlough scheme.
- The Internal Market Bill clears the first hurdle in the House of Commons in the UK. MPs backed the bill in the vote last night by 340 to 263. It will protect Northern Ireland and the rest of the UK if negotiations on a trade deal with the EU break down.
- Aleksei Navalny is recovering in a German hospital from being poisoned and has now been able to get out of bed. He said he will not go into exile in Germany and plans to return to Russia to continue his mission.
- Russia and China have started using experimental vaccines under emergency use measures and are striking international deals to sell their vaccines.

- In the US, Republican leaders in the US Senate said they would vote to advance a scaled back Coronavirus stimulus plan. It is thought to reinstate federal unemployment benefit to $300 per week which is half the previous package.
- Trump finally admits to playing down the seriousness of the virus as he said he did not want to cause panic in the early days of the pandemic!
- It appears Russian spies have been hacking US officials accounts working for both Republican and Democratic campaigns where China seems to have focused on the Biden campaign, according to an assessment by Microsoft.
- With 50 days to go until the election, Joe Biden assembles a legal team to deal with the expected wrangle over mail-in voting and the President's opposition to accept the vote and decision if he is defeated. He has already said he may refuse to leave office. The Biden team has enlisted two former solicitor generals and hundreds of other lawyers.
- The damage to the global economies from the pandemic has been four times more damaging than the crash in 2009. The biggest declines were in India (minus 25.2%) and in Britain (minus 20.4 percent.)

CHAPTER 30

Week Two in September on the Campaign Trail

Thoughts of Lisa Lerer of The New York Times

Following her week's holiday of enjoying perfect weather as the leaves begin to fall, with picnics in the park and beach days, the arrival of lower temperatures and pumpkin spice heralds election season! Even Joe Biden is now out on the campaign trail. With just eight weeks to go, Joe Biden, having avoided plane travel thus far, made a visit to Michigan and put forward his plan for jobs to a small socially distanced crowd in Union hall. By contrast, Trump visited and held rallies in Florida and North Carolina minus social distancing and minus masks.

In Washington, Congress made little progress in passing the economic relief package. This will perhaps have little bearing on the political landscape and/or outcome of the November 3rd election. Over the coming weeks many topics need to be addressed, not least of which is the race to find a reliable vaccine to the Coronavirus. Also, a big concern is the continuing racial injustice protests spiralling into violent protest hailed as right-wing militants. Joe Biden also condemns the violence while supporting the message and the right to peaceful protest concerning law enforcement and the need for change and the Black Lives Matter movements, among others. Perhaps the most topical subject is the voting itself by mail and online. Championed by the Democrats but condemned by Trump, who claims the result will be false/corrupt and has even threatened not to uphold the decision if he is defeated [74]

Another book in the headlines this week is by Bob Woodward on President Trump. There are many revelations in it of course but perhaps the most topical is that Trump admitted downplaying the Coronavirus in an attempt to avoid mass panic. The book, titled "Rage", due out this week, draws on information from a series of 18 private, on-the-record interviews with Trump. Woodward writes of very uncomplimentary description of generals and officials critical of their support of allies. Even as he admitted downplaying the virus, he said he "will always be a cheerleader for the country" and prided himself on saving lives by imposing a travel ban quickly on China. Even as the reports of this book came out, Biden condemned the President once again in a suitable vein for having "failed to do his job on purpose." Rather than, on this occasion, attack the author for the content of the book the President seems to accept he said all those things, which he did, and seeks to defend himself. Possibly to deflect attention from the book the President this week floated a potential list of people he would nominate to the Supreme Court if he were elected to a second term. Those names include three Republican Senators, Tom Cotton of Arkansas, Ted Cruz of Texas, and Josh Hawley of Missouri. Others on the list from around the country include Trump's lawyers, former solicitor general, and State and federal judges. He did this in 2016 although this year perhaps not the same swing votes around Supreme Court judges with other issues on the table. [75]

---

[74] New York Times, by Lisa Lerer.
[75] New York Times; On Politics, Giovanni Russonello.

Round Up of Polls, 12th September 2020

❏ The Cook Political Report: two changes moved Florida from "lean Democrat" to "toss up." Nevada from "likely Democrat" to "lean Democrat."

❏ Trump advisors view Florida as a "must win" for Trump but the change shows Biden's weakness with Latino voters and Trump stabilizing after the months of protest over the killing of George Floyd.

❏ A Monmouth University poll shows Biden holding a seven-point lead over Trump nationwide with 37 percent of registered voters saying they would vote for Trump and 43 percent voting Biden.

❏ NBC/Maris College Survey of Florida shows Trump and Biden tied at 48 percent. But with Trump at 50 percent among Latino voters.

Going into week three in September further snapshots of the huge number of polls currently tell us Trump is holding his advantage on the economy but Biden is holding advantage on virus handling. Trump's predictions of chaos in the suburbs are not getting through. Voters don't care for Trump's line of "law and order" but do believe some of his false accusations against Biden over "policing." The suburbs are key however, though as the Republicans have only lost in those States three times since 1980 (1992, 1996 and 2008.) Democrats won the Presidency on all three of those occasions! [76]

DB 15th to 21st September

❏ Many European countries are finding ways to open up and live with the virus. Masks, social distancing, enhanced hygiene in every setting, and increased testing. Examples of this are seen

---

[76] New York Times; On Politics, Lisa Lerer.

in Spain and Italy. However, in England the cases are growing, and the testing process is in crisis. Many cannot book a test or must travel hundreds of miles only to arrive and find test kits have run out. The Government promises to sort this in a matter of weeks.

- Over the summer European countries seemed to be rising from the economic downturn as the European Central Bank sought to support by lending and seeking to stabilize the economy. However, political concerns over the resurgence of the virus throw that into doubt. Britain is at loggerheads with the EU and could exit on a "no deal", which would impact on the major trading partners such as France, Spain, and the Netherlands. The economy in Britain is further hit by shoppers staying out of the cities, people working from home, and cancelling holidays.

- For the first time since opening in 1958, the Jerusalem Great Synagogue will remain closed over the Jewish High Holy days in Israel due to National Lockdown.

- Thursday sees a warning from the World Health Organisation of a serious resurgence of Coronavirus. The virus has increased in case numbers by more than 10 percent in recent weeks across half the countries in Europe. It is hoped that local lockdowns rather than national can contain and suppress but in Scotland, England, and Wales tougher restrictions are already being imposed. Currently only two households and a maximum of six people can meet indoors or outdoors in any setting, but many local areas are not allowed to visit other households or have visitors inside or outside.

- In France, the rate per capita is the highest in Europe with 91 cases per 100,000 which is up from just 10 per 100,000 in July.

- Aides of the Russian Aleksei Navalny say evidence that he was poisoned in his hotel in Siberia, and not at the airport, has come to light as traces of the poison agent Novichok are found on a water bottle in his room there.

- As the row between the UK and the EU rumbles on, Joe Biden tweets that any deal between the two must not threaten the Northern Ireland peace treaty. It is thought that Biden is at best looking at a lukewarm relationship with Britain post Brexit where Trump has been more favourable with trade talks thus far.
- In continuing unrest in Belarus, security forces arrest hundreds of women. Women have become a huge symbol of peace and often hold flowers and wear white while protesting.
- Britain moves to impose heavier fines for those breaching lockdown rules.
- President Trump on Tuesday hosted President Netanyahu of Israel at the White House along with foreign ministers from the United Arab Emirates and Bahrain for signing of the historic diplomatic accords between the countries.
- The US says it will start to distribute a vaccine within 24 hours of it becoming available and that Americans will not pay to have it.
- Nancy Pelosi is determined not to send lawmakers home from the House until a new round of legislation to save the ravaged economy is passed. She told CBC yesterday (16th) that she would not adjourn the House for November elections until a bill is passed. A group of 50 legislators calling themselves "House Problem Solvers Caucus" later unveiled a $1.5 trillion proposal for the next step of economic relief. Much of it includes areas where Democrats and Republicans are and have been opposed all summer. It is unlikely to pass but does confirm the need for both sides to agree before the November elections.
- The Postal Service yesterday began sending out cards advising voters to plan ahead if they vote by mail. Most States have not yet begun accepting applications to vote by mail and the Democrats saw this as a way to cause confusion early in the process. Some Secretaries of State say they plan to raise

- concerns over the mailings with Louis DeJoy, the Postmaster General, which is scheduled for today (18ᵗʰ).
- In the polls, generally speaking, Biden is holding onto the lead although it is narrowing in some States. If the Polls are as wrong as they were in 2016 it is still likely that Trump would be re-elected. But Biden is leading, and it seems he may hold on to it.
- Ruth Bader Ginsburg, Justice of the Supreme Court, has died 18ᵗʰ September 2020 in Washington D.C. She died from pancreatic cancer.
- President Trump immediately vows to appoint her successor before the election, citing his constitutional right to do so. While thousands hold vigils and mourn her passing, both Republicans and Democrats engage in discussions on who will when her chair will be filled.
- The battle begins over the situation of Trump wanting to nominate Ginsburg's replacement and throws the election campaign into further turmoil. Less of a referendum on Trump and more focused on key issues including of a battle over court and notably issues on abortion and healthcare.
- US citizens who asked for an electronic ballot from abroad should by now have received one.
- Supreme Court Justice Ruth Bader Ginsburg will lie in repose at the Supreme Court this week and if President Trump waits until after the funeral that will leave just 38 days until election. Trump seeks support to nominate her replacement before the 3ʳᵈ of November even though the normal process for approval will take 70 days. Many in both parties oppose this action.
- Judge Amy Coney Barret is seen as the front runner in Trump's choices.

CHAPTER 31

Week Three in September

President Trump is increasingly vocal about his desire to have a vaccine available before the November elections, but many are worried about the safety of such a rushed project and many Americans say they would not have it. Robert Redfield, Director of the CDC, said in a testimony before the Senate yesterday that a vaccine would not be widely available until next year and that the wearing of masks remains a vital part of suppressing or containing the virus which prompted criticism from the President. The President went so far as to say the doctor had made a mistake and that a vaccine would be available "immediately." Joe Biden accused Trump of using the vaccine as a political tool, saying that he trusted the doctor who based his opinion of medical and scientific research and facts, but he does not trust Trump and neither do the American people.

Sadly, but not unexpectedly, Supreme Court Justice Ruth Bader Ginsburg died on 18th September 2020. She had been suffering from pancreatic cancer. Her passing triggers an outpouring of grief across the country and vigils are held as thousands mourn. President Trump vows to appoint her successor before the election which also triggers huge responses from across all political parties and so the conflict begins. Senator Lisa Merkowski said she opposes confirming a Supreme Court nominee before the election. She is the second Republican Senator to do so and Nancy Pelosi, speaker of the House, cast the battle over the Supreme Court seat as a fight to save the Affordable Care Act. Mr

Biden, having spent months condemning Trump's handling of the pandemic, faces the bitter battle over the Supreme Court seat while seeking to link the vacancy to the future of healthcare and the pandemic. The death of Ginsberg at such a time could upend the whole 2020 election. But while battles have long since raged over cultural divides, guns, and abortion, Joe Biden seeks to use this time to focus on protecting the Affordable Care Act including the popular guarantee of coverage for those people with pre-existing conditions. Further Mr Biden has, on Friday, called for the Senate to stop any nomination to the Supreme Court before the election. Mr Trump pledged to move forward without delay. He vows to pick a woman next week. Senator Mitch McConnell of Kentucky and the majority leader vows there will be a floor vote. Senator Chick Schumer of New York, the Democratic leader, urges his Democratic colleagues to make the case that another Trump pick would jeopardise the health law. [77]

Meanwhile, Mr Biden prepares for the first debate which is scheduled for September 29th. He was not expected to announce his list for consideration of nominees to the Supreme Court before election day, but he has vowed to appoint a black woman. Representative Alexandria Ocasio-Cortez of New York and a leader of the Democrats progressive wing said that the motivation is making sure the vacancy is protected for the next President to fill. Worth noting perhaps that Kamala Harris, VP, Senator of California, is a member of the judiciary committee and will serve as an interrogator for whomever Trump nominates. She has already clashed in that roll with Trump, including with both of his attorneys.

Democratic donors poured money in just hours after Ginsburg's death, reaching $80 million in just 24 hours.

---

[77] New York Times: On Politics team.

DB 22nd to 30th September

❏ In the UK Boris Johnson warns the UK has reached a perilous turning point in the fight against Coronavirus. Johnson has been widely criticised for his mishandling of the pandemic and in sombre tones and following press calls from the Chief Medical Advisor and Chief Scientific Officer he sets out tougher new restrictions which could remain in place for six months. They actually reflect the measures Scotland has imposed for several weeks now as England opened up sooner and faster than the other devolved nations. Pubs, bars, and restaurants close at 10 p.m., table service only, and more wearing of masks in public or enclosed spaces with tougher fines for those breaking rules.

❏ In Scotland, the First Minister goes further with restrictions and imposes no indoor gatherings in households with a few exceptions to cover, support bubbles, extended households, couples living apart, and tradespeople. Pubs, bars, and restaurants to close at 10 and restrictions also may be up to six months.

❏ Aleksei Navalny leaves hospital in Germany today, 23rd September. He plans to remain in Germany just now but also will return to Russia to continue his mission.

❏ Prince Harry and Meghan Markle have appeared across media platforms encouraging people to vote. Meghan has long since voiced her political views although while a working member of the Royal family this was not permitted. However, with Prince Harry adding his own words and views and openly discussing politics in America, many in the UK and in America feel he has overstepped the mark. It is possible that Her Majesty the Queen does not see this as them upholding her views and standards. Many in America feel it is none of his business and should not interfere, especially as he has no vote and very limited experience of the country and its cultural, political, social, and racial heritage (BBC/author.)

❏ France raised their Covid-19 alert level after a surge in some areas, and with further restrictions on public gatherings.

❏ Virus cases surge in Europe, causing concern among officials, fearing a second wave and hospitals being overwhelmed. However, the hospital and death rates are not rising at the same rate so far. Possibly younger people are getting mild symptoms. But they will in time pass this on to older generations and they will likely require hospital treatment, and some will die.

❏ In Scotland, the First Minister announces no indoor visits between households and pubs, bars, and restaurants to close at 10 p.m. In England, the 10 p.m. curfew is imposed but two households of maximum six people can visit indoors.

❏ In Scotland, as fresher's week arrives across all Universities, many engage in house parties and cases surge. Hundreds of students in several Scottish Universities test positive after flouting rules. They are all told to stay in their rooms this weekend and not permitted to visit their parents as no households to meet indoors.

❏ Novavax announces it will begin final stage testing of a vaccine in the UK.

❏ The UK government announces a job support scheme to begin when furlough ends. It will support wages to 50% of normal income but only for viable jobs. Some will be lost and those saved will lose 22.5 percent of normal income.

❏ When questioned Mr Trump again casts doubt on his willingness to transfer power peacefully should he be defeated in the election.

❏ As Scottish Universities announce hundreds of cases after students arrive in halls of residence the R rate rises and up to 11% of those tested are testing positive. The student communities across the country are in lockdown as stronger measures kick in across Scotland and in huge areas of England.

- More testing is leading to higher positive cases but hospital rates, although rising, are not leading to the same critical numbers of the peak and deaths remain low. This will change as the spread increases.

- A rare, bright moment for Royalists in the UK arises as Princess Eugenie of York announces that she and her husband Jack Brooksbank are expecting their first baby in early 2021. He or she will be the Queen's ninth great-grandchild. The couple have been married almost two years. Her elder sister Princess Beatrice recently married in a small family service after her planned wedding was postponed by Coronavirus lockdown.

- Monday 28th dawns with the row over UK University resident students showing no sign of abating and opposition parties call for a delay to many English Universities opening. Students however are told they can travel home and must self-isolate with their entire household for two weeks and not use public transport to get home. Isolating means: do not go out, do not have anyone in, and do not go out even to exercise or for food.

- The world is set to reach a grim milestone in the fight against Coronavirus and reach a total of one million deaths. India records the highest daily virus totals, then the USA with Brazil and Mexico third and fourth. These four together account for more than half of the total globally. In addition, 32 million people have been sick, and it has touched almost every country and territory in the world. Britain, Spain, and France are being hit by second waves.

- Winter is coming and flu season sees the vaccination programme in the UK begin.

- The Netherlands imposes further tighter restrictions as their cases soar to high levels once again.

- In the UK, the Prime Minister Boris Johnson gives a press conference to set out the new restrictions around England and local lockdowns. In Scotland, the current strict rules remain in place while differences between the devolved Nations lead to confusion. Many people are finding it tougher than ever as the second wave in the UK takes hold and the winter is fast approaching.

- On Aleksei Navalny, recovering from being poisoned, the question is looming over whether the situation gives rise to Germany taking a tougher stance on Russia.

- Russia's Federal Protective service has built a bubble of protection round President Putin. A photo on news accounts shows him sitting at his desk in a large office conducting Zoom meetings on an enormous screen. It is said that anyone who comes face to face with him must have quarantined for 14 days first. Further there may be a disinfectant bubble at his residence outside Moscow. A strange contrast to his paranoia over Covid-19 given that his government viewed the virus as vanquished!

- As the Coronavirus spread across Europe in late February and early March, Americans, Britons and Germans arrived in Ischgl, a famous ski resort in the Austrian Alps. No one was alarmed but when the skiers and tourists went home they took the virus with them, spreading it quickly to more than 40 countries on five continents. Nine months into the pandemic, which has reached every country in the world, how global tourism collided with the pandemic remains a challenge difficult to control, difficult to treat, and destructive to global economy, health, and welfare in all corners of the world.

- In the US, the death toll passes 200,000. More than in any other country.

- As President Trump achieves the support needed to have a vote on the Supreme Court nominee, it is also noted that the CIA says Russia, or President Putin, continues to interfere with the US election process.

- In the US Johnson and Johnson are ready to enter the next stage of a single-shot vaccine trial involving 60,000 people. It does not need to be frozen so distribution should be eased.
- Thousands of protestors gathered in Trafalgar Square in London claiming Coronavirus is a hoax. This has happened in other cities. Berlin, Brussels, Dublin, and Paris. Bizarre and distressing as global deaths pass one million.
- France, in the grip of a second wave, announces closure of pubs and bars in southern areas of Marseilles and Aix-en-Provence.
- Senate Republicans seem to support whoever the President nominates to the Supreme Court. Perhaps anxious that the Senate may have to rule on the election result and Trump does not want an even number of Justices.
- The New York Times Lisa Lerer runs a story on Friday in which she discusses election stress disorder with Steven Stosny. It seems across America many people argue over election choices even if they agree on who to vote for. It is normal to be stressed in election year but 2020 is exceptionally difficult. Uncertainty, fear, job losses, social problems, financial stress, and of course health can be overwhelming.
- As voting by mail gets started with voter registration day, it is thought 38 million Americans have disabilities and voting this year is more challenging than ever before due to the risks presented by the pandemic.
- On Saturday 26th September President Trump formally nominated Amy Cohen Barrett for Supreme Court Justice.
- The NYT reports on President Trump's taxes, saying that in 10 of the 15 years before he became President, he paid zero tax. It is also reported that in 2016 and 2017 he paid $750 per year. How bizarre! He blames recording huge business losses over the years. A decade-long battle with the IRS continues but if he loses he could face a tax bill of more than $100 million.

- New York City is on the brink of a financial abyss after the effects of the pandemic wreak havoc on the economy and it could take years to recover, maybe even into 2023.

- The much anticipated and first debate between Trump and Biden was painful to watch, depressing, and alarming in equal measure and as both men engaged in personal attacks, lies, and false claims while Trump interrupted constantly, it ended with no winner and the only loser being the American voter. Full story in Chapter 34.

- After Trump's claims that the mail-in ballot will be flawed it seems likely that he will throw the outcome of the election, should he lose, to the courts to decide. Due to the large number of ballots by mail the result will likely not be known until long after the polls close. Maybe even a week.

- Jim Rutenberg has written an in-depth piece for *The New York Times* on his investigation into the Republican party's efforts to suppress voting and strike people from voter registration rolls across the country. His investigation ran for five months. Republicans seek to prove it is unreliable to have the election dependent on mail-in votes where Democrats hold firm on the validity of the process essentially. But both sides are worried, there are major issues, and the biggest worry is of course interference and the continuing impact of Coronavirus on voter turnout. (New York Times)

Another month closer to the US Presidential Election and another month where my plan to note three items of daily news per day has vanished in the scramble to keep up. I thought when I began that I would write for maybe an hour a day! How wrong. Email news pinging in from the New York Times three or four times a day it feels and sometimes I feel I just have to write it down. Early morning, mid-morning, late at night ... it just does not stop.

CHAPTER 32

Jostling for Position in the Polls

A vacant Supreme Court seat reshuffles the election and throws the race into further partisan conflict. And as voter registration day arrives, Americans are already voting. So far the question is, should the Republicans push through a nomination before the election? But the debate over the court brings many other issues into the cause, such as abortion and healthcare. While it is too early to gain a view of what American voters think, there are views from both parties. Republicans welcome anything that shifts the focus away from Trump's handling of the pandemic and an open Supreme Court seat reminds people why they support Trump, drawing the focus to him delivering on his promise to re-make the federal judiciary. But there are issues in this also as we reflect on Republican Senators who refused to agree to an appointment in the election year of Judge Merrick B Garland, Barack Obama's last Supreme court pick. Further, there is the matter of Senator Lindsay Graham, running for re-election this year who said in 2016 "if there's a Republican President in 2016 and a vacancy arises in the last year of the first term, let's let the new President, whoever it might be, make that nomination." As Mr Graham is now pushing for the President to push through his nomination and nobody likes a hypocrite, the Democrats are vocal in their condemnation and visible in their protest. The vacancy plays to one of the Democrats' strongest voting blocks, female, and gives another reason for Trump to delay his nomination until after Ruth Bader Ginsburg's funeral as has now been announced. He has also vowed to nominate a black female. Aides are advising him on the tightrope between courting evangelical and Catholic voters on matters of abortion and not alienating more moderate suburban women who are already defecting to the Biden camp.[78]

On the subject of Coronavirus, it seems even the CDC can't even agree with itself. Having posted on their website that the main transmission route for the virus is through droplets, they have subsequently removed the wording from their website. They said it was an error and will update new guidance soon. Medical experts don't all agree on how it is spread although evidence backs up the aerosol's theory (droplets inhaled). There have been other cases where they have reversed guidance, for example saying that those in close contact with an infected person but who were themselves are asymptomatic should not get tested. This was later reversed as evidence proves asymptomatic people can transmit the virus. *The Times* reports that the confusion came from the first directive coming from political appointees in the administration rather than from the scientists. [79]

Tuesday 22nd September heralds National Voter Registration Day. The process has been moved online, as has everything else this year. The major tech companies are using their reach to sign up potential voters and Joe Biden is holding a virtual rally. Alarmingly perhaps the Brennan Centre for Justice this week said that voter registration rates have plummeted in 2020, declining by an average of 38 percent from 2016 in 17 of the 21 States analysed. Two key battleground States show a drop of two percent in Wisconsin but in Arizona it is down 65 percent. Some advocates say it is down because there is little or no on-street in-person visible campaigning due to the pandemic and a lacklustre interest in the election. Campaigners and outside political groups have focused digitally. Much of corporate America have also joined the digital voter registration push with social media platforms at the

---

[78] New York Times; Lisa Lerer.
[79] New York Times: Giovanni Russonello.

forefront. Facebook announced on Monday 20th that they have already registered 2.5 million voters via Facebook and Instagram tools and platforms. Snapchat added the ability to register and added 400,000. OkCupid, an online dating site, is allowing people who have registered to vote to add a badge "Voter 2020" which claims to increase the chance of getting a message back by 85 percent. Other avenues include celebrities, the music industry, and even a push to register at the cash register, both in person and online. In stores like Foot Locker and outlets like Dover Street Market stores will post signs with a QR code for Smartphone users to scan which takes them to an online registration portal. The QR code is also on receipts issued if you miss the sign initially. Forty states now offer online registration. This could be crucial to the turnout and outcome in this year of the pandemic.[80]

House Democrats reached a deal with the White House yesterday (22nd) which agrees a stopgap on spending measures which seeks to avoid shutdown just weeks before the election. The bill now needs approval from the Senate before going to Trump. Congress has been unable to agree on the broader spending bills that would keep the government funded when the new fiscal year begins on October 1st.

Mitt Romney announces he will support the President in pushing through his nomination which just leaves two Senate Republicans opposing a vote before the November election so it looks certain Trump will be going ahead and he currently plans to announce his pick on Saturday 26th September.[81]

The polls seem to indicate that Arizona, which has been turning blue for some time, could actually flip from red to blue this year. The State has voted Republican every year since 1952 except for one occasion. Bill Clinton won a rare victory in 1996. When Trump won from Hillary Clinton in 2016, he only had 48 percent of the vote. With most pollsters unhappy at the President's handling of

---

[80] New York Times: On Politics.
[81] New York Times: Giovanni Russonello.

the Coronavirus, all views point towards a Biden win. The Pew Research Centre has predicted that for the first time Hispanic voters will be the largest racial and ethnic minority group in the US electorate. Nearly one third of the Arizona population is Hispanic, up one third from 20 years ago. This could have a positive bearing for the Democratic vote. However, exit polls in 2016 showed Mrs Clinton winning Latino voters by about 2 - 1. Joe Biden is lagging a bit but there is definitely room to grow. The gender divide is another pointer to uncertainty as the Latino men under 50 are just as likely to vote for Trump as they are Biden according to Ms Valencia of political strategy firm EquisLabs. [82]

---

[82] New York Times: On politics. Giovanni Russonello.

CHAPTER 33

Amy Coney Barrett

President Trump announced his nomination for Supreme Court at a press conference in the Rose Garden of the White House on Saturday 27th September, not unexpectedly confirming Amy Coney Barrett, conservative, as his choice. Barrett is 48 years old, married, Catholic, and has seven children including two adopted, with her husband who is also a lawyer. She is a graduate of Notre Dame University Law School in Indiana and after graduating there she clerked for the late justice Antonin Scalia. In 2017 Trump nominated her to the Chicago-based Seventh Court of Appeals. Described as a devout Catholic, this makes her a favourite among religious conservatives to overturn the 1973 Supreme Court decision to legalise abortion nationwide. LGBT groups have criticised her for her membership of the group People of Praise whose network of schools have guidelines stating a belief that relationships should only happen between heterosexual, married couples. Judge Barrett has ruled in favour of Trump's immigration and gun rule policies in the past. Conservatives hope she will rule against the affordable care act which is a legacy of former President Barack Obama. 20 million Americans could lose their healthcare if this act is overturned.

Her nomination sparks a bitter fight as Democrats seek to delay her approval, believing that the next President should have nominated the next Supreme Court Justice and the Republicans are set to push the approval through before the 3rd of November election. If Judge Barrett is confirmed then the conservatives will hold a 6-3 majority on the Supreme Court for many years to come. She would be the third Supreme Court Justice appointed by President Trump after Neil Gorsuch in 2017 and Brett Kavanaugh in 2018. Appointments are usually for life so at 48 years of age Barrett has many years ahead! [83]

---

[83] BBC News for US and Canada.

CHAPTER 34

When September Ends

On the eve of the first of the live debates between Trump and Biden, the President faces questions over his tax returns and the *New York Times*/Siena poll puts Biden nine points ahead of Trump in Pennsylvania. Trump only narrowly carried the State in 2016 and the 20 electoral votes available could prove crucial this time round. The first face off will stream live from Cleveland.[84]

The debate! As the debate unfolded (which I watched on catch up on BBC News) it was instantly clear that the previously sober events focusing on policy, legislation, and plans was now replaced by the spectacle of both men hurling insults at each other, with Trump bullying and interrupting Biden, it was a mess. In Lisa Lerer of NYT own words, it left her "disgusted and depressed." Two men in their 70s with little self-restraint moderated by another septuagenarian who was unable to impose any kind of order or basic agreement over rules. Oddly, it was Biden who levelled most insults, hailing the President of the United States "a liar", "the worst President America ever had", "Putin's puppy", "clown", and "racist." And he told him to shut up! It was a mess. However, Trump, who barely let a sentence go unchallenged, seemed to come out "on top". But CNN called it "an avalanche of lying" as Trump launched personal attacks on Biden and his son Hunter and spewed one lie after the other on every subject or statistic he quoted. Even worse perhaps he refused to condemn white supremacy and almost encouraged them, saying, "Proud Boys,

---

[84] New York Times: Giovanni Russonello.

stand back and stand by." Proud Boys, the far-right group who have endorsed violence. saw this as tacit approval. Trump cast huge doubt over the order and legitimacy on mail-in ballot voting, which has already begun and insisted that the result would be rigged and flawed. So insistent on this subject was he that even some Republicans are alarmed that he may be scaring off his supporters from voting by mail-in ballot. With the President trailing in the polls and the general view that Biden won the debate over a wealthy President is leading some to evaluate how the next debate goes forward. The next event is in Miami and the moderator is expected to have new rules in place which allows him to mute candidate's microphone if they break the rules Chris Wallace of Fox news, who was hosting, also struggled to maintain order and was drawn into dialogue/debate by a belligerent Trump. The Debates Commission who oversees such events are planning further adjustments to facilitate a more professional and productive debate next time. [85]

Following the debate, Biden headed to the Amtrak station in Cleveland the next day to begin with a speech and a busy day of campaigning. Trump headed to Minnesota to plan for two outdoor rallies scheduled there for this weekend. However, the area is in the "red zone" and strict social distancing is in place as cases of the virus are at a high level. A strange choice for Trump but he is not known for his love of wearing masks or social distancing. [86]

The second debate is slated for October 15th in Miami. The third is slated for October 22nd in Nashville. [87]

30th September 2020 Campaign funds raised:

President Trump: Candidate Committee Money: $476,324,349.

Outside money: $118,394,412.

---

[85] New York Times: Lisa Lerer.
[86] New York Times: On Politics.
[87] CBS News.

Joe Biden: Candidate Committee Money: $531,009,149

Outside money: $171,332,498.

Total across the campaign: $3,159.6 million.[88]

DB 1st to 7th October

- In Britain cases continue to surge alarmingly with the highest recorded number of cases pouring in over the weekend with hospital admissions, deaths, and the spread to the elderly all rising.
- Big differences across the devolved nations in the number of cases per 100,000 population but the four nations are holding meetings to discuss next steps and it is likely further restrictions will be brought in to those already in place. The Prime Minister wants to keep the economy open but protect lives. The hospitality industry is expecting to be hardest hit now as talk of a "circuit breaker" lockdown is floated around.
- The First Minister in Scotland is likely to announce further restrictions for the country today as numbers of cases continue to rise along with hospital admissions. However, the nation is growing weary and discontented.
- In Britain, the government is forced to acknowledge a massive blunder in the failure of the track and trace and recording of Coronavirus cases blaming computer malfunction of an outdated excel spreadsheet model not equipped to handle the volume of data. It has put lives at risk. Many are furious. Health Secretary Matt Hancock promises an investigation and an upgrade of the computer system.

---

[88] Open Secrets.org.

- Following four nation talks, the First Minister in Scotland is expected to announce new restrictions today to curb the rising infection rate now thought to be between 1.3 and 1.6 in Scotland. Hospitality industries are likely to be targeted. Currently no visitors in each other's homes but can meet one other household up to six people in a public bar or restaurant. Possible travel bans are expected in local regions but promised not to return to national lockdown. The country is fatigued with the indecision and often failure of the national government to be cohesive or decisive.
- 90 British Universities have Coronavirus outbreaks, and many are spreading into the local communities.
- New Zealand is hopeful that the second wave of Coronavirus is now over after 10 clear days of no new cases as the country lifts restrictions and moves forward again.
- In Scotland, the First Minister announces tough restrictions for the whole central belt where cases are rising rapidly but leaves other areas of Scotland in the same restrictions as before, adding that alcohol must only be served outdoors.
- Pubs, bars, and restaurants must close for 16 days from 10th October and only hotels may serve alcohol outside to residents. Gyms may stay open for individual use, but no classes allowed. Casinos, bingo, arcades etc. all to close. It is tough for all (my family lives in the Central Belt) but an effort to drive down infection must be made.
- Early on 2nd October the White House announces that President Trump and the First Lady have tested positive for Coronavirus. Both are said to be doing well. However, by close of business the President is suffering mild symptoms of fever, fatigue, and a cough so is flown in Marine One helicopter to hospital.
- Over the weekend a series of conflicting and confusing reports emerge from the President himself and his doctors. The treatment he is thought to have points to a much more serious

case of Covid-19 than indicated earlier yet the President was seen making a drive-by appearance at the hospital. He waved, wearing a mask and in a suit. It is branded a foolish action and puts his security and team at further risk.

- Late on Monday 5th October President Trump leaves hospital and returns to the White House. He removed his mask in a show of defiance and urged Americans "do not be afraid of Covid."
- The President ends talks on the proposed stimulus package for the economy and to help many struggling Americans. Congress is in dismay and the stock market plummets.
- The Vice President debate made history as Kamala Harris, the first woman of colour on the ticket, went head-to-head with Mike Pence. However, no clear winner and less drama than the Presidential debate last week.

CHAPTER 35

Trump Tests Positive for Coronavirus

Early on 2nd October the White House announces that both the President and the First Lady have tested positive for Coronavirus. Initial reports are that they are well and have mild symptoms and that the President remains in power, in charge, and working. The task of tracing his contacts over the last week is extensive and the President's habit of not wearing a mask and holding indoor rallies is likely to have spread the virus. His closest aide in the White House has also tested positive. The Vice President and those down the chain of command, should Trump become too ill to work, are tested and found to be negative at this point. By close of the day the President is flown by Marine One helicopter to Walter Reed medical centre and treated with a cocktail of experimental drugs. The President is 74 years old and considered high risk as he is overweight and has an underlying but common heart problem. To say that this puts the election up in the air is an understatement.

What happens if the President is too ill to remain in charge?

He can hand power to the Vice President Mike Pence until he considers himself well enough to take back control.

Chain of Command: Vice President Mike Pence, and he has tested negative so far. Following him it would be the Speaker of the House, Nancy Pelosi, who has also tested negative so far. If the President was to remain too ill to work some things are clear but other situations more clouded. The Constitution is clearest if a President dies, or must resign from office, for example too ill to continue after being incapacitated. The 25th Amendment states that in this case the Vice President shall become President. This has happened eight times, most recently in 1963 after the assassination of John F. Kennedy when Lyndon B. Johnson became President. Also, in 1974 when Gerald Ford became president after the resignation of Richard M. Nixon. The Constitution leaves it to Congress to decide what happens if the Vice President also dies or cannot serve and several laws have been enacted to lay out the contingencies. At this point it is not urgent to pursue further scenarios as the President may recover in full within a week. Briefly though, after the Speaker responsibility is passed to president pro temperature of the Senate and then members of the cabinet, starting with the Secretary of State. Current Speaker, Navy Pelosi, is aged 80 and the current president of the Senate is Senator Charles E. Grassley, Republican of Iowa and is aged 87!

Further, the Amendment grants the Vice President, acting with the cabinet or a group appointed by Congress, powers to intervene. If a majority of either group decides and informs the House and the Senate that the President is unable to discharge the powers and duties of his office, then the Vice President shall immediately assume the powers and duties of acting president. This action has never been used and may prove difficult to do so now.[89] But it would last until the President informed congress that "no inability exists" and he could perform his duties. If the group disagreed the decision would be left to Congress with a requirement that two thirds of the House and Senate must agree in order to strip the president of power. Whatever unfolds it is a historic moment in US politics.

However, the issues raised by his illness at this point in an election campaign are far reaching. Reporters in the political team at NYT are experiencing an unprecedented time of challenge and nobody can know what happens next. Immediate issues are the rescheduling of the debates, the postponement of rallies, or

---

[89] New York Times: On Politics.

allowing them to go ahead without Trump and the campaign team running the show. Biden for sure will continue with his campaigning although kind messages of support were immediately sent to the President and First Lady for speedy recovery and the Democratic campaign is removing all negative ads aimed at Trump. The question of the Supreme Court appointment may also be in flux now. For now, though 3rd October, even in hospital, the President remains in power and in charge.[90]

Over the weekend various reports emerge and we hear from the President himself. It is evident that the virus has impacted much more than we were told. The President has had oxygen after his levels fell below the normal. He has had steroid treatments and drugs which would normally be used in the treatment of more severe cases. He put out a video message saying he now "gets it" and "understands more" while also embarking on a drive-by at the hospital to wave at his supporters. He was wearing a mask and suited in the back of his limousine. It is possible the President is driving his own treatments without being fully aware of related risks or he could just be trying to prove a point that he is recovering. Either way, the drive by put his team at risk. Mark Meadows, White House Chief of Staff, was reluctant on Friday to acknowledge the gravity of the President's illness initially. A huge exercise to trace those he had been in contact with rumbles on with many already traced testing positive. It is thought the event hosted at the White House following the nomination of Amy Coney Barrett has become a "super spreader" event. However, Mitch McConnell, the majority leader who was forced to suspend the Senate's return for two weeks as Senators test positive, has vowed to go ahead with Barrett's confirmation hearings. Polls continued to show that the President had slipped further after the debate with Joe Biden but obviously were conducted and reported before the announcement of Trump's diagnosis. Next up to consider is the VP debate between Mike Pence and Kamala

---

[90] New York Times: On Politics.

Harris which has taken on a whole new perspective while the President remains in hospital and at a critical point in his journey through Covid-19.[91]

On Monday 6th October President Trump leaves hospital although still having treatment for Covid-19 and, at his physician's words, "not out of the woods yet." He arrived back at the White House in suit and tie, removed his mask, and declared that people should not fear the virus and get on with their lives. The confusion and misinformation surrounding the whole question of the President's health is worrying for many Americans. The world is watching in a country which has seen the President hospitalised with a serious illness in the final stretch of an election whose result he has already said he won't accept if defeated. Infections in the White House and in Congress grow daily, potentially stalling government matters and all while the country faces a pandemic, struggling economy, and social unrest amid racial tensions and dealing with Russian interference in the election! National Security experts fear the country is seen as weakened or distracted and real threats exist. The White House needs, now more than ever, to step up the pace. [92]

Ad campaigns through the President's illness shifted slightly. The Trump camp bowled ahead with negative ads attacking Joe Biden while the Biden campaign removed all negative ads and focussed on a positive spin promoting Kamala Harris, almost as if she was number one on the ticket. The upcoming debate between Harris and Pence from Salt Lake City, Utah, on Wednesday is front and centre right now. They will be debating 12 feet and 3 inches from each other and although offered flexi screens Joe Biden declined them, heralding them as unnecessary. [93]

---

[91] New York Times: Giovanni Russonello.
[92] New York Times: Lisa Lerer.
[93] New York Times; On Politics.

VP Debate 7th October 2020, Salt Lake City, Utah

The debate between Kamala Harris and Mike Pence went ahead as planned with the participants socially distanced, maskless, but with a fairly useless flexi glass panel between them. The feeling from *Times* reporter Lisa Lerer is that it all seemed quite ordinary even though the times we are living through are far from ordinary. The two went head-to-head on healthcare, economy, abortion, climate change, foreign policy, and the Supreme Court. Both largely avoided questions and gave little or no answer to anything significant. Historically VP debates do little to change voter views but the third party in this election, the Coronavirus, commands everyone's attention. Harris fared better on this subject, perhaps because she went straight to the attack saying, "the American people have witnessed the greatest failure of any presidential administration in the history of our country." Pence really only countered her assault on Trump's handling of the virus by saying things could have been worse! He then tried to convince us that Biden's handling of the pandemic would have been worse which is baseless speculation. In the end he had little to say other than to call for "comity", pleading that the American people come together and support Trump. There is little "togetherness" around under a President who constantly inflames voters' feelings with his constant barrage of Tweets. In an otherwise dull debate, the highlight for social media seemed to be when a fly landed on Pence's head and he carried on regardless. [94]

DB 8th to 15th October

❏ Spotlight on Sweden today where the taxation system is currently 57 percent and prides itself on providing top health care and other extensive government services including a year

---

[94] New York Times: Lisa Lerer.

parental leave and cash assistance for those who lose their jobs. The deaths from Covid-19 however have come from the most vulnerable in the population, the elderly and many in the care sector feel the government has failed to protect them.

❏ After six months France, Spain, and Britain are in the grip of second waves, and all are struggling to find a balance to protect life with local, tiered, or total lockdowns, all while keeping the economy open to protect jobs, economies, and balance the growing debt of each country.

❏ European Union foreign ministers on Monday agreed to impose sanctions on President Lukashenko of Belarus following months of unrest over the dictator's re-election in August. He is already under sanctions from the US, Britain, and the Baltics but in retaliation he has expelled several ambassadors of EU member states.

❏ England, Wales, and Northern Ireland are all set to impose further and stricter lockdown measures in an attempt to slow the spread in the second wave. Scotland is currently largely locked down already but the review in 10 days is likely to extend current lockdowns with an extra three-tier system in place depending on case numbers regionally.

❏ The Commission on presidential debates announced that the next debate between Trump and Biden would be virtual due to Covid concerns. Almost immediately Trump says he "will not waste his time" and dismisses the idea.

❏ Joe Biden offers to attend a televised Town Hall meeting instead of the debate Trump dismissed. The Democrats share of the vote in the polls is 52%, which is rare at this point in campaigns.

❏ Trump declared Kamala Harris "a monster" which Biden condemned, saying he clearly has issues with strong women and Mitch McConnell, Republican leader of the Senate, said he has avoided the White House for months due to the lack of masks and social distancing in place there.

- The latest *New York Times* investigations into Donald Trump's tax returns found that more than 200 countries, interested groups, and foreign governments had patronised the President's properties, bringing in millions of dollars while reaping benefits from him and his administration.
- The latest CNN polls show that Trump is trailing around 16 points to Biden and that there has been no sympathy bump from his Coronavirus episode.
- President Trump is back out on the campaign trail, holding rallies attended by thousands.
- Judge Amy Coney Barrett was sworn in with her family supporting her in Washington on Monday for the first day of her Senate confirmation hearings. Republicans all likely to vote yes for her and the Democrats will vote no.
- Hearings continue for Amy Coney Barrett and she evades some questions and follows precedent on others by refusing to be drawn on how she will rule over specific questions such as healthcare, abortion, and rulings asked for over the Presidential election.
- Dr Fauci spoke out against Trump holding large outdoor rallies, with the crowd largely maskless, no social distancing, and said it is just "asking for trouble." The President's performance was bizarre.
- As Trump continues on his campaign trail many press teams are wary of covering due to the risk to themselves as the President and his entourage do not practice safe distance, masks etc.

I have tried to streamline the "brief" and look more at the election musings as the big day draws ever closer.

CHAPTER 36

The Home Stretch and Turbulence

A current hotspot in this point with Covid is in Wisconsin which is also a key battleground state where Trump only squeaked ahead in 2016 by a small margin and is looking to face a challenge this year to even hold on to that. In one poll it looks as though voters are placing more thought on his handling of the pandemic than on economy, healthcare, and on his judgements on social problems.[95]

Ed Rollins, a long-time Republican operative who is now a super PAC supporting President Trump, has admitted "it's an uphill battle." The Republicans seem to be in disarray with Trump trailing in national polls and in some battleground States, his disastrous Presidential debate, and the White House becoming a super spreader of Coronavirus! Mystery still surrounds his own episode with the virus; when did he first test positive, how ill was he, and is he fully recovered? Just three weeks to go and some now feel even in Republican camps that he can't turn it round and that they may even lose the Senate. Democrats are raising huge sums of money, notably $57 million collected by Jaime Harrison, the Democrat challenging Senator Lindsey Graham of South Carolina. Most political forecasters are now saying the Democrats are likely to take control of the Senate.[96]

---

[95] New York Times; On Politics.
[96] New York Times; On Politics.

DB 15th to 22nd October

❏ In Scotland, the First Minister announces no change to the household restrictions currently in place and confirms that on 26th October no guarantee of any return to normal or reopening of pubs, bars, and restaurants. But a new three-tier approach on level of alert related to cases and deaths similar to that in England will be introduced along with a further 20-million-pound package of help for business and low-paid staff.

❏ Cases continue to surge across Europe and some countries, such as France, bring in curfews. France curfew is 9 p.m. until 6 p.m.

❏ With France in the grip of a second wave of virus, President Macron is struggling to grasp control as hospitals are becoming overwhelmed.

❏ Across Europe countries are also struggling as cases have risen from six to seven million in 10 days with a daily death total hitting 1,000 for the first time.

❏ It is announced today that Wales will go into a national lockdown for two weeks from Friday to try and curb the surging virus. Scotland has huge parts of the country already in stricter lockdown than in places where numbers are lower but fatigue, frustration, and uncertainty over the winter months and Christmas is leading to worry and many, many problems. In England, the Prime Minister has introduced a three-tier system of lockdowns, trying to balance human lives with economic recovery for the country.

❏ In New Zealand Jacinda Ardern wins a landslide election victory and another term in office. New Zealand's most popular Prime Minister in decades and perhaps ever!

❏ In England, the Mayor of Greater Manchester Andy Burnham has been warring with the government who seek to put the 2.8 million people into the strictest lockdown. He asks for more financial support as it will devastate the jobs and families in the area. Are jobs in the North being sacrificed to protect the more affluent South?

- In the last day of hearings for Judge Amy Coney Barrett the affordable care act takes centre stage. There were points when the Judge's view leaned towards leaving the ACC intact.
- Democrats are trying to portray Barrett as an extremist but presenting an image as some kind of super Mom in twinset and pearls is thought to try and defuse that.
- The US Justice department announces indictment of 6 Russian Military intelligence officers over interference in the 2016 election.
- NBC will host a Town Hall style meeting with Trump at 8 p.m. opposite the same event with Joe Biden on ABC. It is therefore impossible for Americans to watch both events live.
- The feedback on the Town Hall meetings were perhaps predictably with Trump standing at a lectern, combative, desperate, and engaging in a war of words even with the host and Joe Biden by contrast seated and engaging in a more political, orderly discussion.
- Trump appeared to confirm that a suggested $400million debt was a small amount of his claimed net worth and that none of it was owed to Russia.
- Joe Biden admitted that he would change the number of Supreme Court Judges but declined to answer what number he has in mind if elected President.
- In America, across Europe, and around the world, Coronavirus surges and combined with people's fatigue over ever-growing restrictions, job losses, economic gloom, and uncertainty over vaccines or a route out, many are struggling to stick to rules while frustrations grow in others as a result.

- Speaker Nancy Pelosi tries again to broker a deal for virus relief and said maybe an announcement from the White House in 48 hours is possible. If not, then it's unlikely she can help get relief passed before election day.

- No stimulus package has been agreed since Spring and poll show voters strongly wanting Congress to pass a bill by election day. Senate Republicans are reluctant to pass a big stimulus package until the election result is known. Senate majority leader Mitch McConnell may hold a vote this week on a $500 billion bill which is way short of what Democrats demand.

- In the next Presidential debate, due on Thursday this week, some rule changes have been made. Subjects are Coronavirus, race, leadership, "American Families", national security, and climate change.

- The US Justice Department announces indictment of six Russian military intelligence officers over interference in the 2016 election, interference in 2018 Winter Olympics, the French presidential election, and Ukraine's power grid

- Trump calls Fauci a "disaster" and claims people are tired of hearing about the virus. Voter registrations in three key States for Republicans offer hope to them in Florida, North Carolina, and Pennsylvania.

CHAPTER 37

Trump Trails

The polls continue to show Trump trailing as he occasionally looks desperate and pleading for votes. As half a million of Americans have already voted on ballot papers, what do we know today? Well, President Trump and Senator Thom of California are trailing, signalling potential trouble both for the Presidential election and for the Republican control of the Senate. The *New York Times*/Sienna poll also has Biden leading Trump among likely voters at 46 to 42 percent. Biden's standing in North Carolina, a State Trump won in 2016, is consistent with the leads he has built in other battleground States. Early in-person voting begins in North Carolina today, 15th.[97]

As we head into the weekend of 17th/18th October, the polls are showing Trump trailing with not much time left to recover. Since the Presidential debate on 29th September one poll showed Trump with a slight edge but the University of Georgia/Atlanta Constitution poll now shows a clear seven-point Biden lead in a Quinnipac University survey released on Wednesday. Overall, they show Trump failing to match the support he had in 2016 and notably in white college graduates and older voters. The effects are spilling over into Senate races with Mr Ossof in one, challenging Senator David Perdue, having narrowly lost a 2017 special election for a House seat in the Atlanta suburbs. In the Quinnipac survey Ossoff led by six points, yet in another Perdue has a sizeable lead. Another wide-open race to fill the seat left vacant by former Senator Johnny Isakson

---

[97] New York Times: Lisa Lerer.

Democrat Dr Warnock consistently gathers most support in polls although he faces two Republican candidates who combined have more support. If no candidate wins 50 percent in either of these two races, as is likely, a runoff would be held in early January. If trends continue as the polls show, then next month Joe Biden could be in a position to carry Democrats 2018 gains even further and with suburban voters too. As early voting by mail ballot continues, the pollsters face many challenges to predict as there are many known problems with the early mail-in ballot system and many predicted. For example, in Georgia, there will likely be long queues, and some will give up and go home without voting. Hour-long wait times are ten times more likely to occur in heavily black areas compared to white. And always the possibility that many will turn up to vote and find their names purged from the roll. In one analysis it is thought the 2017 purged 100,000 names who would otherwise have expected to vote. The polls could also look to past voter behaviours, but this is an election like no other before it and huge variance in predicted results and actual results are expected.[98]

At this point, while many hope for a Biden victory, I personally think it is too close to call. I have spoken to friends and family in the United States, and I have spoken to friends and family at home. I have listened avidly to the BBC News teams and Washington correspondents. Some, of course, are just wanting to see Mr Trump depart from the White House but for strong and loyal Republicans it is difficult. The more Democrats I speak to or listen to on TV and in the newspapers the more I sense a hope that Joe Biden may actually be elected. For the Republicans though it is very difficult. It is very close, it is very unpredictable, and I expect many bumps in the road before any outcome. [99]

While the polls continue to show Biden leading there is of course, according to many, a nagging voice saying, "what about 2016?" The same thing happened with Hillary Clinton. only to have Trump

---

[98] New York Times; Giovanni Russonello.
[99] Sally Foster.

steal it and so begin four years of American history. However, according to NYT reporting both Trump and Clinton were the "most disliked and polarising Presidential candidates in American history." Trump's inflammatory rhetoric and Clinton tarred by decades of Republican attacks and facing the inevitable, perhaps, sexism as the first women to have a serious shot at President. Focus groups found Clinton condemned by younger groups of women for staying with her husband after his infidelities and older women doubted their own ability to break down barriers and believed she couldn't do it either to become the first female in the White House. But 2020 is not 2016 and most see Biden as a "decent family guy." Her ratings in polls of 2016 showed her unfavourable rates at more than half with 10 to 15 percent very unfavourable higher than Biden this year. Only about a third saw her as trustworthy where in 2020 Biden sits around 52 percent "favourable." And Trump is trailing so still the polls point at a Biden victory. An election like no other in the midst of a raging pandemic, widespread voting by mail, and record shattering early voting all making this difficult to call.[100]

DB 23rd to 31st October 2020

❏ The First Minister in Scotland, having extended the current restrictions across the country to November 2nd, will announce later today the five-tier plan going forward and we are told to prepare for a "digital Christmas."

❏ Spain announces a state of emergency and tough restrictions which could last all the way until May 2021 as they reach their highest number of daily cases ever. A 1 p.m. until 6 a.m. curfew is in place to limit movement. However, the Canary Islands, where cases are low, is unaffected.

---

[100] New York Times; Lisa Lerer.

- Three months after the alleged corrupt election of Alexander Lukashenko in Belarus, unrest and protests continue.
- The Scottish government announces five tiers for the way forward living with Coronavirus and tried to align with the UK government's five-tier plan in England. Cases of Covid continue to rise and some hospitals are close to capacity, especially in some parts of England and in the west of Scotland.
- In Britain, the NHS braces itself for the next six months as hospitals fill with Covid-19 and non-essential operations are delayed. Many feel that they need more staff, more funding, and more PPE as the second wave intensifies, with differing strategies across the four home nations leading to this being a longer and more sustained wave than the first and that was bad.
- French President Emmanuel Macron announces a one-month full lockdown will start on Friday 30th October as the country is seeing huge rising numbers of cases and medical services are becoming overwhelmed.
- Germany is similar and Chancellor Angela Merkel announces further closure of restaurants, bars, gyms, theatres, museums, and beauty salons for one month.
- The UK NHS announces that no visitors will be allowed in any sites with exceptions for next of kin if patient is end-of-life, dementia, mental health patients, and partners of those giving birth.
- The economic impact in Europe continues to be felt as shares drop to their lowest level in months. A long, dark winter lies ahead for the UK and Europe, the US and almost every other country. It is hard and yet still many in my home country continue to break rules, protest against governments, and hail the virus as a hoax. Tensions are rising in families, friendships, mental health is suffering, routine medical care and services are suffering and still the case numbers rise, people are dying

and those who recover can be left with lifelong life-changing aftereffects.
- ❏ Drug maker Sanofi and GlaxoSmithKline have vowed to provide 200 million doses of a potential Covid-19 vaccine to an international coalition designed to give countries equal access to Coronavirus vaccines.
- ❏ Across Europe many countries are having to impose stricter measures to curb surging cases of Covid, but all are keeping schools open with tougher measures in place. It is a lower risk as children are thought to be at less risk and there are much fewer cases in the young universally.
- ❏ In Britain, former Labour party leader Jeremy Corbyn is suspended over allegations in an anti-Semitism row highlighted in a report issued by the Human Rights watchdog which saw him deflect blame. Investigations to follow.
- ❏ In France, two weeks after a teacher was killed for mocking Muslims in class, three people were killed in a knife attack in a Church in Nice. France is increasingly at odds with the Muslim communities both at home and in other countries.
- ❏ In a much calmer debate, due to the "mute" button, the final Presidential debate took place in Nashville Tennessee which saw Trump hail Biden as an ineffectual Washington insider and Biden accuses the President of being heartless for separating migrant families and inflaming racial tensions.
- ❏ The Republicans advance Barrett's Supreme Court nomination although the Democrats boycott it. The Judiciary Committee has set up a vote effectively, on Monday, to confirm Judge Amy Coney Barrett to the Supreme Court.
- ❏ On Monday evening the Republican majority voted to confirm Amy Cohen Barrett to the Supreme Court. No Democrats voted and probably the first time the minority party has not voted. Cohen will sit to rule on key issues, notably mail-in voting issues in three battleground States within days.

❏ Early voting has surged with large numbers already casting ballots across record numbers of States for this point in the election. Roughly 70 million votes cast. This is more than 50% of overall turnout in 2016!

❏ On Thursday both Trump and Biden arrived at court votes from this key battleground, possibly deciding State. Neither man was confident, and continued with their opposite styles of campaigning from loud, in-person rallies from Trump to quieter, safer, drive-in rallies from Biden.

CHAPTER 38

The Final Countdown and Supreme Court Nomination

With the vote to appoint Judge Amy Cohen Barrett to the Supreme Court set for Monday, there is much discontent among Democrats. Her all but certain appointments will shape American justice matters for decades as appointments are for life usually and she is 48 years old. Sweeping implications for corporate power, environment, gay rights, and abortion, plus many more, come with Amy Cohen Barrett and all just eight days before the election. Furious Democrats spurned the vote and forced Democrats to waive their own conditions of requiring at least two members of the opposition to be present to transact business. The boycott and majority-only vote to recommend the nominee marked a new precedent. There will be more battles to come over the Senate now.[101]

While the debate remained orderly, it is unlikely to give Trump the bounce he seeks in swing States where he is still trailing. But more worrying perhaps for him is that the Trump camp has a lot less money to spend in the final week of campaigning than the Biden camp. Such is the crisis that Trump has slashed his television ad budget for campaigning and diverted from swing State campaigning last week to California to seek cash injection. He has also started an online onslaught, sending many emails each day soliciting cash injections. Joe Biden's camp entered October with $177million to

---

[101] New York Times; Nicholas Fandos.

Trump's $63.1 million and is leveraging that up just as Trump seems to be looking for money. Yet another problem for Trump in this beleaguered election process. [102]

In the final presidential debate Biden, in the face of Trump's assault on him as a career politician and being ineffective in Washington, remained unmoved by the attack and stuck to his own agenda for the war of words. Biden leads now by around nine points while Trump trails, similar to figures in 2016 against Clinton but he has made some inroads into key parts of this election. Some strength for Biden comes from the low opinion of many of the President's handling of the pandemic which has become such a defining part of the election and in shaping American lives going forward. The President even now reckons that after he is re-elected nobody will talk about Coronavirus and yet the US reaches record numbers of infections and deaths each day. The result of the election remains unpredictable but before the debate 48 million people had voted and Trump is pushing hard for a last-minute red wave to help him pass the post. But all things point to growing strength for Joe Biden as we reach the penultimate weekend before 3rd November with 54 million now voted and so many more in the next 10 days or so. [103]

A story circulating since the last debate which the President hoped would trouble Joe Biden appears to stutter to a halt. The story that Joe Biden, former Vice President, had known about and profited from his son's business activities in the Ukraine was touted to the Wall Street journal by the Trump camp but failed to gain any traction and therefore failed to get the President what he wanted from it. It was perhaps a last-ditch attempt to deflect the campaign from the Trump negatives and focus on Biden's negatives instead. NYT Daily brief.

Entering the last week of the campaign now there is still little evidence of energy or visibility from Joe Biden. President Trump

---

[102] New York Times; Shane Goldmacher and Maggie Haberman.
[103] New York Times; Lisa Lerer.

has hosted rallies in Pennsylvania, a key swing State, and then went on to host an event at the White House to celebrate the confirmation of Amy Cohen Barrett to the Supreme Court. Contrastingly, Joe Biden spoke for barely 10 minutes in Chester Pa, just over the state line of Delaware (home state) and was last minute, and attended by a small group of reporters. When questioned by reporters on a lack of campaigning or visibility in the last week arose, he was a little defensive. He has visits planned this week to Georgia and Florida. While Trump is highly visible and noisy, Biden seems to be drawing a contrast that he is quiet and steadfast and definitely not another President Trump. But, of course, Trump pounces on this and this week has accused him of, "being a pathetic candidate …" However, Biden has been overwhelming Trump in ads on the airwaves. Casting himself as the sober and responsible candidate he chooses not to travel the country for fear of spreading the virus and attempting to show Trump as irresponsible for travelling and holding outdoor rallies for thousands and all this after the White House was and still is a super spreader of the virus. An unrepentant President touting that after the election we won't hear any more about the virus even as the US records its highest daily cases and deaths since the pandemic began. If Biden's strategy of being responsible and low key wins him the White House, then his strategy will be seen as smart but if he loses his bid for the Presidency then he may face even more fury from the Democrats than Clinton did in 2016. The position in the polls still shows that even if they are as wrong as they were in 2016 then Biden would still win the White House. NYT/Lisa Lerer. But there are so many unpredictable factors, particularly with the huge number of mail-in votes and record numbers voting it is impossible to call. It is also the case that a result is likely to be delayed due to counting mail-in ballots. The President will resist all delays and has also declared he will dispute the result anyway if he loses. An upfront and noisy Presidential campaign versus the Statesmanship of the challenger who seems to just want to "stay out the way" is a risky strategy and one which not all Democrats endorse. Equally, many Republicans feel Trump is taking too many risks with health and safety and not respecting the virus. We could second guess, watch polls avidly, and count votes already in but the reality is simply that in this unprecedented election campaign, anything is possible. NYT/On Politics.

31st October 2020 Campaign Funds raised:

Donald Trump: Candidate Committee money: $595,630,157

Outside money: $267,922,092

Joe Biden Candidate Committee money: $937,673,077

Outside money: $441,263,961

Total by all candidates: $3,692.6 million.[104]

Coronavirus cases recorded in the US 31/10/20:

9,318,653 and 235,182 deaths recorded.

Coronavirus cases recorded in the UK 31/10/20:

989,745 and 46,229 deaths recorded.

World cases: 46,018,022

Deaths: 1,195,616.[105]

DB 1st to 3rd November

❏ The virus is out of control and hospitals will be overwhelmed in a matter of weeks without this action. Furlough is extended.

---

[104] Open Secrets.org.
[105] General Media Sources.

- Scotland enters the new five-tier system of restrictions, and a row erupts over funding for Scotland if it does not follow the English lockdown. The First Minister seeks clarity from the Prime Minister that should Scotland require more funding for lockdown later, then it would be available. The PM said in Parliament that it would be.
- I live in the Central belt in Scotland outside Edinburgh, and we are in tier three. One example is that pubs, bars, and restaurants may re-open and serve food and soft drinks, no alcohol, and must close at six p.m. Other parts of Scotland are also in tier three and a few in tier two with very few in tier one. No area is in tier four as yet and no areas are in tier 0 which is the closest to normal without a vaccine, we are likely to get in this country. No indoor visitors allowed.
- Violence erupts in Vienna just as nationwide lockdown restrictions are imposed. In what is described as a "terror attack", gunmen open fire in six locations around central Vienna, killing two and injuring fifteen. Police shot and killed one of the attackers, but others remain at large on Monday night (2nd Nov).
- In February, a team of investigators from WHO arrived in Beijing to investigate how Coronavirus jumped from animals to humans. Nine months, 1.1 million deaths later, and still no transparent or independent investigation. China did not allow WHO team members to investigate the source or even visit the market in Wuhan where the outbreak began. The team have ceded control of the investigation which has seen China extract concessions that delayed important research and avoid a potentially embarrassing review of the government's early response to the outbreak.
- England's lockdown comes under fire for loopholes, and many are flouting rules while businesses try to stay afloat.

- Late on Saturday evening, the Prime Minister in the UK, Boris Johnson, announces that he will put all of England into lockdown on 5th November.
- The Bank of England pumps £150 Billion into the economy in Quantitative Easing aimed at shoring up business, jobs, and economy.
- In the last final push of campaigning by both Trump and Biden, the highways resemble the high seas with plenty of drama!
- Joe Biden began his final push in Pennsylvania with a drive-in rally. Trump plans to hold a rally in Scranton, perhaps just to needle Biden.
- Trump has also travelled to key swing States of Michigan, Iowa, North Caroline, Georgia, and Florida, seeking support in the last hours as polls still show him trailing, a seemingly consistent state of play for him and yet he is buoyant in his rhetoric at rallies, as is Joe Biden.
- In Texas, where voting has passed the total for 2016, the Supreme Court threw out an effort to purge 120,000 ballots that had been cast at drive-through locations in Harris County which is heavily Democratic. The suit, filed by State Representative Steve Toth and activist Steve Hotze, alleged that the Harris County Clerk, Chris Hollins, had acted illegally by setting up sites without approval by the State Legislature.
- In Texas over the weekend Trump supporters drove at a Biden tour bus and forced it to slow almost to stop, yelling abuse at it and forcing them to cancel two events as a result of disruption. Trump, far from condemning, hailed their actions as patriotic. Federal law enforcers fear that an escalation of this type of unrest could spring from a contested election result.
- Before polls open on 3rd November more than 96 million Americans have voted. It is likely to lead to the largest ever voter turnout. It is thought huge numbers of Democrats have

voted which may be swaying the polls, but huge numbers of Republicans have held back to head to in-person polling today.

DB 4th to 11th November 202

- A man who opened fire in Vienna, killing four and injuring 22 people, had previously been arrested for trying to join ISIS and was known to Austria's intelligence forces. The gunman was shot dead after nine minutes of his attack.
- Across Europe many countries are imposing strict lockdowns, including travel bans.
- In England, the month-long lockdown begins and the First Minister of Scotland, Nicola Sturgeon, considers a cross-border travel ban to become law to prevent further spread while many hospitality venues ask people not to travel from England or more locally if in a different tier. Furlough is extended.
- On Armistice Sunday Britain holds a scaled down, socially distant service at the Cenotaph in London with the Queen and Royal family members in attendance and representatives of the Military, the Clergy, and Commonwealth, and all who took part in the World Wars and conflicts. A two-minute silence is observed, and people of the UK are asked to stand in respect on their doorsteps both today and on the 11th of November at the 11th hour.
- Biden opposed Brexit and now the UK Prime Minister has a problem with last ditch trade talks with the EU. A trade deal with the US just got more complicated as Biden has already ruled out any deal with the UK if they make a deal with the EU which threatens the protection of the Northern Ireland peace/withdrawal agreement.

- Italy imposes a stricter lockdown as virus cases surge. It will include restricting travel between regions and covers five regions at the moment.

DB 4th to 11th November 2020 – Results in the US

- Votes are cast, counting begins, and Donald Trump is already declaring victory while nowhere near gaining the required 270 electoral college votes. Trump 213, Biden 220.

- Trump continues to trail on 214 electoral college votes after Biden hit 253, winning Wisconsin and Michigan. Trump files lawsuits to stop ballots being counted. He threatens to take the case to the Supreme Court. Americans brace themselves for Civil unrest. Edging towards a Biden win but not a peaceful transition of power and could still end up a draw!

- Counting mail-in ballot papers continues with Biden edging ever closer to victory with Georgia and Pennsylvania close to calling in his favour. If he wins in Pennsylvania, he will pass the 270 electoral college votes required.

- Saturday sees Biden win in Pennsylvania and the NYT calls the race over and the new President-elect to be Joe Biden. He later takes Nevada and sits at 279 Electoral College votes to Trump's 214. It is over but Trump refuses to concede and vows to fight on.

- Now on 10th November and we are still waiting for the remaining four states to declare and still waiting for Trump to concede. He vows not to, and Russia and China so far have not congratulated the President-elect.

- Joe Biden says he will re-enter the Iran nuclear deal, renew a nuclear arms treaty with Russia, and double down on American commitments to NATO. He seeks to reverse the four-year mantra of "America First."

- ❏ President Trump's defeat sees Israel's Benjamin Netanyahu on the receiving end of a demotion in US priorities as Biden has promised a more balanced approach to the Israel-Palestine conflict.
- ❏ While President Trump continues to resist the election result and block transition, refusing to meet President-elect Joe Biden, at a hearing of the Supreme Court yesterday at least five Justices supported the healthcare law. Suggested that striking down the individual mandate, the requirement to obtain insurance, would not doom the balance of the law.

CHAPTER 39

The Vote!

It is 1930 hours, November 2nd, UK time as I write, and pretty much all is now said in this account of the Democratic Primaries which grew and grew as the pandemic unfolded. Here we are with unimaginable case numbers in the US, the UK, and in every country and territory in the world. All eyes, however, are focused on the events to follow as polls open on 3rd November in the US. Never has there been a more difficult time to have a Presidential election. With polls showing a Biden victory and an incumbent President vowing not to accept a result if defeated, along with the inevitable delays of counting mail-in ballots, this is going to be an election like no other! God bless America. [106]

Tuesday Morning – 3rd November 2020

Polls open and the world watches. There are record turnouts across the country as Trump and Biden watch and keep whipping up support in various locations. Major news agencies position themselves in relevant points and in the UK the BBC finally picks up some decent coverage.

---

[106] Sally Foster.

Wednesday Morning Dawns

Trump has won in Florida, which is a blow for Biden, but he has made other predicted wins. By 8 a.m. UK time it is too close to call with 40 out of 50 states declared. Trump is doing better than expected and even takes to the podium in the White House to say he has already won, that the election is fraudulent and that he will go to the Supreme Court to fight for his victory. The votes are not counted, the election is not won by either man yet. Of the 270 electoral college votes required to win, Trump has 213 and Biden 220. Biden takes to the microphone to say he believes he is on track to win the White House. [107]

As Wednesday progressed, Republicans won Senate races in Alabama and Iowa and flipped at least six house seats giving them a net gain in that chamber so far. Democrats also picked up Senate seats in Colorado and Arizona and we waited for North Carolina, Georgia, Michigan, and Maine to be called, which should be Democrat pickups. The waiting continues as millions of ballots are still to be counted and it is only halfway through Wednesday (UK time.) Biden is hopeful and Trump is still calling for a halt to counting votes. [108]

Moving into Wednesday afternoon and evening Biden takes Wisconsin and then Michigan and now has 253 electoral college votes to Trump's 214 with 71 remaining. As the margin of win in Wisconsin is just .6%, Trump has called for a recount as he is of course entitled to do. And he has filed a lawsuit to halt Michigan's count. Those two key wins added to his slim leads elsewhere could propel him to the Presidency. [109]

So as Wednesday ends in the UK, there is still no clear result in America and the world must wait. There is frustration across America, uncertainty and unease as a close race is exactly what

---

[107] BBC News UK.
[108] New York Times; Giovanni Russonello.
[109] New York Times.: On Politics.

they did not want. No landslide for either side and a divided country. Fears grow for civil unrest whoever wins, and many businesses have already boarded up windows. [110]

Thursday 5th Dawns

The overnight position sees Joe Biden on 253 electoral college votes and Trump on 214. Millions of ballots still need to be counted. If Biden can win two more swing States, then that may be enough to win even without a win in Pennsylvania. But Trump could still achieve a draw if Biden doesn't make the gains he needs. All to be won or lost but perhaps not even today as the Trump camp persists with legal challenges. With 71 college votes still undecided and three of them in Alaska, expected to go to Trump, the remaining ones of Nevada, Arizona, Georgia, North Carolina, and Pennsylvania will decide the election. If Biden wins Pennsylvania the race is over. If Trump wins Pennsylvania, Nevada, North Carolina, and Arizona while Biden takes Georgia then it will be a tie. That would produce 269 electoral college votes each as the founders created a system that would end up with an even number of Electoral College votes. This scenario is unlikely but not impossible and right now it is easier for Biden to win than Trump. [111]

Later, Thursday 5th

Nothing changes as the vote count continues with no states declaring and the margins remain very tight and too close to call.

---

[110] BBC News UK.
[111] New York Times: Lisa Lerer.

Friday 6th

As counting trails through the night and a new day dawns, the margins remain tight in remaining states and by afternoon (UK time) Biden has edged ahead in Georgia and more importantly in Pennsylvania which would, should Biden win this, propel him past the 270 electoral college votes. Counting continues, Trump rhetoric continues, and Biden stays calm and maintains dignity. In Pennsylvania, a judge threw out Trump's attempt to halt the counting of ballots but did allow poll watchers to move to six feet away to monitor the process. Trump maintains that ballots not yet counted are illegal. He said, "if you count the legal votes, I easily win." Some remain loyal but even among his own supporters he seems to be more isolated in his rambling and outlandish claims.[112]

The count continues all through Friday_with little change in predictions and no results declared, although Biden continues to pull ahead.

Saturday 7th

As the count goes on with still no declaration, unrest springs up; there is impatience across the country and President Trump goes to play golf at his resort while Biden maintains dignity and speaks quietly and confidently of victory. Finally, late on Saturday afternoon (UK time) it is declared that Biden has taken Pennsylvania and secured more than 270 electoral college votes. The *New York Times* and other news agencies around the world declare the new President-elect as Joe Biden. Trump immediately refutes it and disputes it. Later, Biden also takes Nevada, propelling him now to 279 EC votes to Trump's 214. Alaska, Arizona, Georgia, and North Carolina are still to declare. However,

---

[112] New York Times; On Politics.

celebrations begin, and Joe Biden prepares to deliver his first speech. The first task in hand is to head to Washington and prepare to form a team to head up handling the Coronavirus. In his first address as President-elect Joe Biden seeks to soothe the divisions that defined the last four years in US politics. Kamala Harris acknowledges the historic nature of the election, saying, "While I may be the first woman in this office, I will not be the last."

Joe Biden Speech

Speaking on Saturday night in Wilmington, Delaware, and five days after the election and almost exactly 48 years since he was first elected to the Senate during which time he ran for President three times, Joe Biden was greeted with an explosion of car horns and cheers and he seemed almost surprised by the outpouring of celebrations. He had finally arrived. He thanked his supporters, he warmly praised Kamala Harris, and was in this dark time relentlessly optimistic and encouraging; "We can do this," he said. "Let this grim era of demonization in America begin to end here and now." A line that people will talk about long into the Biden presidency. He largely ignored President Trump, naming him only once, and didn't refer to the fact that he had not conceded (as he should have done) and neither did he comment that many top Republican leaders had not congratulated him. He reaffirmed, "The people of this nation have spoken ... They have delivered us a clear victory, a convincing victory, a victory for 'we the people', we have won with the most votes ever cast for a presidential ticket in the history of this nation – 74 million." [113]

---

[113] New York Times: On Politics.

CHAPTER 40

The Final Result

By the morning of 8th November little has changed, and the result is not fully declared or confirmed as ballots are still to be counted. President Trump of course remains in office until 20th January and continues to resist the result. He is perhaps now at his most dangerous, both in America and around the world. The peaceful transition of power is simply not going to happen. I had anticipated that the last chapter would have a nice clean concise ending with the new President declared. It will be a few more days before all results are in and the way forward will be fuzzy until then. But one way or the other, this story will conclude and the new study of the "The First Hundred days" will begin! We are now already on day five though ...[114]

November 10th – Where are we now? First Hundred Days and Counting

While the vote count continues and America emerges from nearly two years of campaigning, two dozen presidential candidates and close to $14 billion spent, America remains a fiercely divided country with no concession from the defeated President and a President-elect beginning transmission. This is the first hundred days like no other. Both men gained more votes than ever before

---

[114] Sally Foster.

with Biden hitting the most votes in history and Trump the second most. Much has changed but the priority, much as before the election, is still the Coronavirus pandemic. The US crossed 10 million cases with new cases up 60% in two weeks, millions more unemployed, and families slipping into poverty daily. The Senate is not like it was when Biden worked there before and is, like America, more ideological and more polarized. Dual victories in Georgia's run off early next year would give Democrats the tie-breaking vote in the Senate but split control with Mitch McConnell remaining as majority leaders is more likely. Republicans hold tight in the Senate and on the Senate floor McConnell declined to recognise Biden as President-elect. A country so divided it cannot even agree that the President-elect has been chosen.[115]

With the Trump administration continuing to ignore the election result, and votes still to be counted, it is not possible to write a clear definitive ending to this story. Therefore, as much as I had hoped to write Part 2: The First 100 Days as a stand-alone – as it happens diary I will continue JOURNEY TO THE WHITE HOUSE until the last ballot is counted and Trump concedes! Rather than report daily, however, in the format of a Daily brief on the US, Coronavirus, and events around the world, the eventual part two will be solely focused on Joe Biden's journey to the White House, which will inevitably blend US politics and issues of fighting the pandemic, restoring the economy, securing healthcare plans, dealing with world leaders, and looking at Brexit and climate change and take a broader view on a week-by-week basis. I hope that all who read this story of history as it happened will get a feel for the vastness of the difficulties the whole world has faced in 2020. After a virus, originating in Wuhan, in a live animal market, far from the shores of the US and the UK where I live, infected the whole world and in turn the difficulties we are all facing, just as announcements of vaccines being available around the world in

---

[115] New York Times; Lisa Lerer.

time for Christmas emerges. On this eleventh hour of the eleventh day of the eleventh month, as we remember the fallen from World Wars and conflicts around the globe, we continue to fight an unseen enemy like no other. [116]

They shall grow not old, as we who remember them grow old. Age shall not weary them, nor the years condemn. At the going down of the sun, and in the morning, we will remember them.

---

[116] Sally Foster.

CHAPTER 41

Mr President Meets The First 100 Days!

Overview of 12th to 19th November

President-elect Joe Biden announces his Chief of Staff to be Ron Klain, who worked alongside him as his Chief of Staff when he was Vice President to President Obama. Klain first worked for Biden in 1989 after graduating from Harvard Law School while Biden was a senator from Delaware. Like his appointment of Kamala Harris as his VP, it is no surprise to note that Biden plans to bring his closest people to the White House administration. The concern grows even among Republicans at Trump's continued refusal to accept defeat and acknowledge Biden. Lawsuits are being filed and dismissed as the vote count continues and many feel that the transition, particularly on planning how to manage the pandemic and all other matters of Federal Government, should be taking place. Outgoing President Obama in 2016 met in the White House with Trump on 10th November to begin the process. As world leaders begin to congratulate the President-elect, Britain's Prime Minister has a 20-minute call to do just that, and no doubt Brexit comes up in conversation. Johnson is still locked in bitter negotiations with Barnier over the trade deal and with Biden's self-proclaimed loyal ties to Ireland making it clear he will not trade with the UK if Ireland is compromised in Brexit, Prime Minister Johnson is walking a tightrope. Biden has also received congratulatory calls from national leaders in Asia, Europe, and Australia. He is, of course, in absence of any transition, having to use non-secure phone lines, which he would have access to if Trump would do the right thing. There is still no sign of that.

Joe Biden has also spoken to Pope Francis, who he thanked for "promoting peace, reconciliation, and the common bonds of humanity around the world." Biden, who is only the second Catholic to be elected President, pledged to work with the Pope to fight global warming and to care for the "marginalised and the poor."

Also, this week, James Lankford, a Republican Senator from Oklahoma, told a radio interviewer that he would step in to make sure Biden had access to daily briefings if the President was still not making them available by the end of the week.

Finally, by the end of the 13th of November, 10 days after the election, all the votes are now counted with Arizona and Georgia going to Biden and North Carolina going to Trump. [117]

The electoral college result is decisive with 306 to Biden and 232 to Trump.

It is over! Now, surely it is time for Trump to accept that and concede? Not so, even as several Senate Republicans insist that Biden should at least be given access to the President's daily brief which provides the nation's most closely guarded secrets and an assessment of national security threats. Their call seems to indicate acceptance that Mr Biden would be certified as the victor in the election. Democratic leaders warn that Trump failing to concede and accept defeat is damaging the country's ability to deal with foreign leaders, and the process of planning and handling the most high-risk period of the spread of Coronavirus as it continues to surge in record numbers, and with Thanksgiving on the horizon, concerns are growing nationwide. More Republicans are beginning to acknowledge the result and accept Biden is going to be the new President, including Gov. Mike DeWine of Ohio and veteran party operative Karl Rove, along with an editorial in the Las Vegas Revie Journal which is a newspaper owned by the

---

[117] New York Times: On Politics.

family of Sheldon Adelson, who is a huge campaign donor. [118]

Today I read from my usual sources of New York Times *and the* BBC News UK *that Roy Blunt, a Missouri Republican and member of the Senate leadership, said he agreed that Biden should have some details of briefings, including matters of national security. While most of the G.O.P have not yet acknowledged that Biden won the race, their comments are showing how they see it in reality. But other Republicans have stopped playing along with Trump's claim that the election results are in doubt. Mike DeWine, Republican governor of Ohio, accepts Biden as the winner as does Karl Rov,e publishing an article in the Wall Street Journal titled "This election won't be overturned." Chuck Grassley, when asked, said that Trump should accept defeat by December 13th, one day before the Electoral College delegations will cast their votes for President. As I write it is December 14th here in the UK.*

Trump may privately acknowledge defeat as he is already talking of running for President again in 2024. Clearly removing Trump from the Oval Office will not keep him out of the news cycle. He got a huge number of votes; the margins were tight and the predicted landslide for the Democrats did not happen so this President, it seems, will not go quietly. [119]

Over the weekend and into the beginning of week commencing 16th November, President-elect Joe Biden begins to take steps to structure policy for a government no longer under Trump control. Trump is of course still in denial even though many leading Republicans continue to fall in behind others that transition needs to begin in the best interests of the country and, more importantly, national security.

News from the UK sees Prime Minister Boris Johnson self-isolating seven months after he battled Coronavirus as he has been contacted through track and trace as being in contact with a person with a positive Coronavirus test. Later in the day other

---

[118] New York Times; On Politics.
[119] New York Times: On Politics.

members of the government are contacted and asked to self-isolate after further positive tests emerge. Will he have antibodies? We must wait and see! This could not have come at a worse moment as tensions still exist over Brexit and the gap between the EU and Britain over trade deals is now pointing towards a "no deal", which both sides want to avoid. It is thought that Biden also favours a deal as he is known to favour Ireland in all Brexit negotiations.

Joe Biden's first speech on policy again calls on President Trump to begin a peaceful transition and he reaffirms his strong views on mask wearing and how it can help slow the spread of the virus. He also spoke out against many of Trump's advisors who have criticised those States who have imposed stricter restrictions to try and contain the virus.

It feels bizarre to me that anyone can criticise efforts to tackle the virus as it is relentlessly surging through America and in many countries around the globe.[120]

Joe Biden names further White House staff; Mike Donilon, who is chief strategist for the campaign and long-term friend and advisor, and Representative Cedric Richmond of Louisiana who will oversee public outreach. Joe Biden is seeking climate-ambitious candidates to fulfil posts across his cabinet. Looking for agencies not necessarily at the forefront of environmental policy, such as departments of Justice, Agriculture, and Defense. Early executive orders could include a revival of the Obama-era mandate that every agency incorporates climate change into the policy.[121] Fifteen days after the election, and after around 30 lawsuits filed by Trump's camp and thrown out by lawmakers, there is no evidence of fraud anywhere. On November 7th, when most media outlets called the election for Joe Biden, Rudy Giuliani declared "It's a fraud, an absolute fraud." But on 17th November, under questioning from a federal judge in Pennsylvania and under oath,

---

[120] Sally Foster.
[121] New York Times; On Politics.

he said, "This is not a fraud case." There are countless other instances where the Trump camp have made false accusations of fraud and so far all have been dismissed. Trump would have to reverse results in several swing States and overcome a deficit of around 45,000 votes across the three closest States. Donald Trump and his supporters cannot change the outcome of the election. Mr Biden will be the next President. [122]

By mid-week on 18th November the US reaches a grim milestone, having suffered 250,000 deaths related to Coronavirus. With no clear strategy from Trump, it is likely to continue at around 2,000 deaths per day, more than any other country around the world. The only glimmer of hope on the horizon is the announcements of vaccines being available by the end of this year. Pfizer and Moderna have accelerated testing and signs are good. But massive distribution and logistical problems loom as well as the nagging doubts over how safe it can be with such limited testing and what are the long-term effects. In Berlin on Wednesday, police were forced to break up protestors who rallied against government legislation underpinning the efforts to constrain the virus. France becomes the first European country to pass two million infected cases this week but are optimistic that strict measures in place are beginning to slow the spread. Jordan, which was initially hailed for a good effort in containing the virus, now becomes one of the hardest hit countries in the region, alongside Iran. In the UK Boris Johnson announces an ambitious "Green Industrial Revolution", music to Joe Biden's ears perhaps and a clear sign that the UK seeks good relations with the President-elect.[123]

Joe Biden begins to turn up the pressure to have transition begin properly as little co-operation has been forthcoming. He quoted the law which says that if the General Services Administration has a person who recognises who the next President is then transition

---

[122] New York Times: Lisa Lerer.
[123] New York Times: Natasha Frost.

must begin, and they must have access to data and information from the incumbent government. He is pushing for the GSA's Emily Murphy to announce officially that he has won. Until then his hands are tied. In a call to supporters yesterday, Joe Biden also acknowledged that he would face difficulties achieving his agenda on many things if he did not win a majority in the Senate. The fate of this rests with two runoff elections in Georgia in early January. Biden pushes ahead while Trump continues to demand recounts and files lawsuits. In other news, the Democrats re-elected speaker Nancy Pelosi as their leader on 18th November.[124]

20th to 27th November

The severe restrictions across Europe appear to be working to reduce the spread of Coronavirus. The vaccine being tested by AstraZeneca and the University of Oxford sees promising results. Hopes begin to rise across Europe. In Denmark, where an outbreak of Mink-related Coronavirus saw a cull of Mink, the government was left with a political crisis as Ministers of Agriculture were forced to step down, leaving the government facing collapse.

As the weekend approaches, Trump summons Republican members of the Michigan Legislature to the White House as he tries to subvert the Electoral College process. Joe Biden condemns this action as sending dangerous messages on how democracy works. Boris Johnson pushes his green plan in the UK as Brexit talks carry on in stalemate, signalling not only his intention to work with the US but around the world post Brexit. As the new week begins, word comes that Joe Biden is going ahead with appointing his cabinet. He will likely choose Anthony Blinken as Secretary of State, Jake Sullivan as National Security advisor, and John Kerry in charge of climate. Other announcements are sure to follow, however, if the two Democratic Senate candidates

---

[124] New York Times: Giovanni Russonello.

in Georgia do not win their January run-offs then Biden will become the first President to take office with the opposition controlling the chamber which could mean trouble for him as he seeks to confirm his cabinet appointments.

After many weeks of delays, Emily Murphy, Administrator for the General Services Administration, finally designated Joe Biden as the winner of the election, providing federal funds and resources to begin formal transition. President Trump accepts the decision and instructs his team to co-operate and do what needs to be done but vows to continue his fight to prove the election results are wrong and defiantly saying he will be proven right. [125]

On the same day, 23rd November, and not long after the Covid-19 vaccine is hailed a success for Pfizer in the US, Boris Johnson is buoyed by the announcement of a British-led Coronavirus vaccine. And, as he sets out the plan for a three-tier strategy after the current month-long lockdown in England, it finally looks as if infection rates are falling – slowly. He begins to talk about plans to allow some relaxing of restrictions over Christmas and is hoping for a four-nation approach. But Scotland remains cautious, and many are fearful of any relaxation. We will pay for it in the New Year with another wave and, ultimately, deaths. In the US, as Thanksgiving approaches, more than one million travellers passed through US airports on Sunday (22nd Nov). This will likely add to the spread of Coronavirus cases. [126]

On 25th November in the UK, it was announced by the Prime Minister that restrictions will be eased for five days over Christmas. So, between 23rd and 27th December Britons from up to three households will be able to travel across the four nations and gather indoors round the Christmas tables. Restrictions however will still apply in hospitality venues, although the three-tier strategy will be in place. The First Minister in Scotland has already confirmed that she will likely curb some of the plan and

---

[125] New York Times: Natasha Frost.
[126] New York Times.

limit how many people may gather indoors and not allow a day at either end for travel to or from Northern Ireland as is allowed for the English. Nicola Sturgeon also stresses that you should only travel and meet indoors if absolutely necessary and urges people not to do it. With a vaccine on the horizon, it is better to keep going as we are and not cause the inevitable spike in January and February this free-movement plan would bring. Meanwhile, in the US, 6.4 million doses of the Pfizer vaccine will be shipped out in the US in an initial push in mid-December. An unexpected emergency authorisation has made this possible. As Thanksgiving approaches, it looks as if only around 27% of people plan to dine with others outside their own household. A virus surge that started in the Midwest appears to be surging in many other places including Baltimore, Los Angeles, Miami, and Phoenix, and first-time surges are being seen in smaller cities. It is quite simply everywhere. In the last week more than 1.2 million cases have been identified in the US and the country will soon hit 13 million cases. The seven-day average of daily deaths is around 1,600. Thanksgiving could add to the tragic figures.[127]

Joe Biden and Kamala Harris formally unveil six top members of the foreign policy and national security team this week and they are all from the Obama era. Speaking in Wilmington, Delaware, Joe Biden said that the team "embodies my core belief that America is strongest when it works with its allies." Linda Thomas-Greenfield is Biden's pick to become ambassador to the United Nations. However, as Biden assembles his team he is also having to try and unify a factious party as the young progressive wing has no interest in a return to the Obama years. Representatives Alexandra Ocasio-Cortez and Ilhar Omar, along with Rashida Tlaib, became the first House members to sign a petition urging Biden not to name Bruce Reed, his former Chief of Staff, to lead the office of Management & Budget. After Senator Diane Feinstein announced she would give up her position as top Democrat on the

---

[127] New York Times: Natasha Frost.

Judiciary committee, the young progressives who wanted her ousted now also want a say in her replacement. Senator Richard Durbin of Illinois is tipped to take top spot but the Senator Sheldon Whitehouse of Rhode Island who is seen as a friendlier ally to the left is the more favoured choice by the progressives and he has also indicated he would not rule out running for top spot. Election results are still being certified and this week[128] Pennsylvania, Nevada, and Minnesota all confirmed for Biden and 36 votes across them while North Carolina certified 15 votes for Trump. Also, this week the stock market soared to record highs as the President-elect's victory was confirmed and Janet Yellen was nominated by the President-elect as Treasury Secretary. Trump tried to claim the rise in the market was all down to him, but investors were responding to the final news of election victory for Joe Biden. [129]

---

[128] New York Times: Natasha Frost.
[129] New York Times; Giovanni Russonello.

CHAPTER 42

Thanksgiving on 26th November to December 3rd

Over the weekend, and as November ends, Scots celebrate St Andrew's Day. In other news, it seems that lockdowns in Britain have exposed a gender gap in sports. We have seen that in English Youth Soccer in particular only a handful of clubs have kept spaces open for girls and yet boys play on.

British regulators may approve AstraZeneca and Pfizer BioNTech before the US. It is thought the vaccines may be rolled out to the most vulnerable in December sometime. Meanwhile, the US federal health officials are predicting a surge in the virus post-Thanksgiving weekend. In a continuing split in Democrats, President-elect Joe Biden is set to name his remaining Cabinet officials very soon. As Christmas looms around the world, many shops are trying to inject some hope and festive cheer by using bright lights and sparkle in their windows. In New York Macey's window is lit up and thanking essential frontline workers.[130] The BBC reports that over Thanksgiving, President-elect Joe Biden has fractured his foot while playing with his dog. He will have to wear a boot-type brace for several weeks.

Boris Johnson is facing unrest from his own party as many are calling for less stringent limits on hospitality as England comes out of the month-long lockdown. It brings little change as they enter a

---

[130] New York Times: Natasha Frost.

three-tier system and most of England will be in the top tier which is just as strict as lockdown and sees some 55 million people in tier three. Scotland, Northern Ireland, and Wales set their own restrictions, but most are in tight restrictions as they try to drive down infection rates and deaths before allowing a "five-day Christmas travel" window. News of Biden's final cabinet picks still trickles out and he seems to be trying to assemble a "diverse liberal-leaning" team of long-time Democratic figures to guide the country forward and out of recession. He has, however, announced an all-female White House staff led by Jennifer Psaki, another Obama-era choice who will serve as Press Secretary. Symone Sanders will be chief spokeswoman and senior advisor to Vice President-elect Kamala Harris. On the last day of November Joe Biden and Kamala Harris finally get the briefings they should have had already. Briefings are conducted in person with a different intelligence official assigned to each person to be briefed. Each presentation is tailored to the individual receiving it and future briefings will be tailored according to their responses and focus on their individual remits and responsibilities. Thoughts also begin to turn to what an Inauguration Ceremony looks like in a Pandemic and Joe Biden forms a Presidential Inaugural Committee. The Committee is led by Toney Allen, President of Delaware State University. It will no doubt look different but Allen vows to uphold and ensure inauguration traditions and engage all Americans while keeping everyone safe.

In other news President Trump discusses with his advisors on whether to issue pre-emptive pardons to a number of people in his inner circle. He fears they may be prosecuted once he leaves office and the list includes three of his children, Donald Jnr, Ivanka, and Eric Trump, his son-in-Law Jared Kushner, a White House senior advisor, and his lawyer Rudy Guiliani.

Joe Biden introduced his economic team on 1st December and urges Congress to act on a stimulus package before he arrives in office. Senator Mitch McConnell, the majority leader, holds firm to the line of refusing to allow a Senate vote on the $3 trillion stimulus bill passed by the Democrat-controlled House. No change in the views from either side looks imminent.

In a world first on 2nd December, the UK gives emergency authorisation to Pfizer's Coronavirus vaccine. Hospitals have already begun scheduling appointments to roll out the first vaccines to hospital, health care, and care home staff starting on Monday 7th at 7 a.m. in London. Welcome news although some are concerned of its safety. Governments, scientists, and advisors hail its effectiveness and safety. Pfizer will ship 800,000 doses in the coming days with a total of 40 million doses on order. Each patient will have two doses, one month apart.

In a move which will turn up the pressure on Senator Mitch McConnell to bring a stimulus bill to the floor, Democratic leaders throw their support behind a $908 billion compromise bill proposed by bipartisan Senators. President-elect Joe Biden endorsed the bill while saying it would not fix everything, but it would be a quick and immediate help for a lot of things and many people. Mitch McConnell opposes spending this much and pushes forward with Republican proposal for a stimulus bill about half this size. [131]

---

[131] New York Times: On Politics/Daily Brief teams.

CHAPTER 43

On to Christmas and Inauguration

Speaking in an interview on 4th December on CNN with Jake Tapper, Joe Biden outlined a couple of intentions once he takes office. He plans to ask Dr Fauci to stay on in the same role as Chief Medical Advisor to continue the fight against Covid, as he has held for many presidents. Dr Fauci has said that Britain has rushed through the Pfizer vaccine and that it's not safe. British governments dismissed his claim and confirmed the stringent testing and authorisation. In America, the Food and Drug Administration are looking at distributing this one if it proves safe in their opinion. Joe Biden also said he will ask all Americans to wear a mask for 100 days after inauguration. On the same day Kamala Harris' team announced Tina Flournoy, a former top aide to Bill Clinton, as her chief-of-staff. Flournoy will lead a team of mostly women of colour. Harris' transition office also announced on 4th December Rohini Kosoglu, who was her chief-of-staff in the Senate, will serve as her national security advisor. [132]

Over the weekend British Prime Minister Boris Johnson prepares to engage in further talks with the EU in final attempts to reach a deal. Ursula Von der Leyen and Boris Johnson have a long way to go in resolving key differences over fishing rights, state aid, and of course Ireland. It is in the interest of both sides to strike a deal otherwise tariffs will be imposed, and the UK will trade, as in the Australia agreement, with the rest of the world. Prices will go up, quota will be compromised, and inevitably delays at ports for

---

[132] New York Times; On Politics.

goods coming into the UK. Painful compromise is needed though, and the clock is ticking. Meanwhile, in the UK, the first vaccinations are taking place with the Pfizer-BioNTech vaccine beginning on Monday 7th December in a world first with the elderly, the highest risk categories, and hospital, medical and care home staff, and residents. It will be rolled out to those shielding, elderly, vulnerable and work from elderly to the younger over months as new doses of the vaccine arrive in the UK. All four nations hope this will have a huge impact on the fight against Coronavirus and begin to give us all some of our previous lives back, more freedom, and begin to rebuild our economies. The National Health Service has taken on retired health care workers and tens of thousands of first-aid workers to assist in administering the vaccine. This is the largest task the NHS has faced. Transporting and storing the virus and setting up locations as clinics is a huge logistical operation. [133]

Meanwhile in the US it seems that President Trump's administration declined to order additional rounds of the Pfizer vaccine when given the opportunity months ago, leaving the United States waiting behind other countries that made the deals. The FDA Pfizer-BioNTech vaccine will be administered shortly but they have only reserved 100 million doses which will cover a mere 50 million people, so around one in six Americans (two doses per person are required). However, other vaccines are being looked at and are in the trial stage. On the Presidency landscape, Joe Biden is expected to nominate retired Gen. Lloyd J Austin III as Secretary of Defense. He is a former commander of the American Military in Iraq. If confirmed by the Senate he would become the first African American to hold the position. In making this choice Biden has skipped the previous expected pick of Micele Flourney, from the former Obama administration who drew fierce opposition from the left. Also, Mitch McConnell still has not agreed to open Senate debate on a stimulus package. So, in the meantime,

---

[133] New York Times: Daily Brief teams.

Congress must prepare to vote on a stop gap package that would keep the federal government funded for another week as it moves towards a stimulus deal and the House is expected to hold a vote tomorrow, 9th December. [134]

With just 44 days until Trump must leave office, he still does not accept his fate as he headed to Georgia, hosting rallies to gain support for the two significant run-offs in January. In a rambling and lengthy speech, he claimed the Georgia State Governor could reverse the results "if he knew what the hell he was doing!" He had called Kemp earlier in the day, but the Republican governor made it clear that he will not be going along with the President's demands to call the state legislatures into session and to subsequently appoint new electors which Trump believes would let the Electoral College deliver the 16 votes from the State when the Electoral College convenes next week. State law is clear, and Trump's demand is not lawful. Attempting to retroactively change the election result would be unconstitutional and lead immediately to court challenges.[135]

On the subject of vaccines in America, regulators are frustrated at AstraZeneca's reluctance to release information and approval for the vaccine hangs in the balance. This of course puts lives at risks as delays can cost lives. Poor communication and delayed drug trials have added to the problems. Meanwhile, in Britain, where the Pfizer-BioNTech vaccine is being rolled out, two people among many thousands have had an allergic reaction. Both carried adrenalin pens and suffer from severe allergies, but some people are now being cautioned if they suffer from severe allergies. Both recovered fully and quickly. Canada has now approved the same vaccine for people over age 16 and will begin rolling it out in the coming week. The United Arab Emirates became the first country to approve a Chinese vaccine thought to be 86% effective and could herald a new opportunity around the

---

[134] New York Times: Giovanni Russonello.
[135] New York Times; On Politics.

world for other countries to use this vaccine. On the transition position in America, a so-called safe harbour is arrived at as the date has now passed where state election challenges such as recounts and audits must be completed. State courts are very likely to throw out any further challenges which come in now.

Joe Biden is thought to be about to appoint Katherine Tai as the head lawyer for the House Ways and Means Committee. If so she will be the first woman of colour in this role. Her experience in the House includes helping to establish bipartisan agreement on the North American free trade agreement last year, previously working for the Office of the United States Trade Representative from 2007 to 2014 where she successfully prosecuted several cases on Chinese Trade practices at the World Trade Organisation. However, Biden is believed to see her focus being on enforcing existing agreements and on integrating Biden's agenda, including fighting climate change and promoting "Buy American" programmes into US trade policy around the world.[136]

Here in Britain the Prime Minister meets Ursula Von der Leyen to once again try and find agreement for a deal following Brexit. Both sides are optimistic, but it is quickly apparent that the most likely outcome is no deal. Britain agreed to drop parts of legislation which would have allowed the government to override aspects of a Brexit withdrawal agreement designed to avoid a hard border Northern Ireland which is part of the UK and Ireland which will remain in the EU. But still Boris Johnson says the offer from the EU is unacceptable. Essentially the EU wanted Britain to accept decisions they make on trade going forward and if Britain refused then sanctions and punishments would be applied. Boris Johnson said no Prime Minister could accept such a deal.[137]

As the week closes on Friday 11th December with Brexit in deadlock, the EU leaders in Brussels agree a stimulus package with member states of €2.2 trillion after lengthy negotiations with

---

[136] New York Times: On Politics.
[137] New York Times; On Politics. BBC reporting UK.

Poland and Hungary which had held up the process. The compromise reached will tie the funding to rule of law standards, such as an independent judiciary and transparency in spending, two principles which had weakened under Poland and Hungary's liberal governments, but the agreement watered down these measures. With the deadline for a Brexit deal now set at Sunday 13th, the European Commission have published no-deal contingency plans. This is an attempt to prevent widespread chaos on both sides on 1st January 2021. While America hopes for a vaccine roll out imminently, it is reported that wealthy nations representing 14% of the global population have bought 50% of the available vaccines. Hoarding in this way must surely be to the detriment of other countries. [138]

12th to 19th December

The biggest vaccine roll out in US history kicks off this week after approval of the Pfizer-BioNTech. Around 2.9 million doses of the vaccine are arriving on a shipment to be sent around the country over the next week. At the same time, major airlines including United, Jet Blue, and Lufthansa are planning a health passport app to record vaccine status and test results for Covid-19 before flying. Bahrain approves a Chinese vaccine against Coronavirus following the path of United Arab Emirates.[139] Over the weekend talks continue between the negotiating teams of UK and EU where we are told both sides "will go the extra-mile to gain a deal." However, Boris Johnson warns that "no deal" remains the most likely outcome and the government announces its plan for this scenario. How to keep supplies moving in and out of UK and European ports. How to ensure the supply chain of vital medicine is not interrupted, limit the impact on "just-in-time deliveries", and

---

[138] New York Times: Natasha Frost.
[139] New York Times: Natasha Frost.

of course shipments of the vaccine must be free moving. Possibly the worst time for the UK to separate from the EU amid the pandemic and economic crisis but there is no turning back and no further delays. Transition period ends 31st December. The vaccine is being rolled out and Christmas looms with an expected spike in cases following a five-day nationwide window allowing free travel between the four home nations and three households to meet up indoors with maximum 12 people. [140]

Some statistics are now emerging on the Coronavirus vaccine roll out. The wealthiest countries have laid claim to more than half the doses coming on the market throughout 2021. Poorer nations struggle to secure enough. If all those doses are fulfilled then the EU could vaccinate its residents twice, Britain and the US four times over, and Canada six times over, according to data analysis. So, in the developing world some countries could vaccinate 20 percent of their populations in 2021 with some not reaching the vaccinations until 2024. In many cases, the US made their financial support for development of the vaccine conditional on getting priority access and are in fact heading to approve a Moderna vaccine this week. Britain has claimed a total of 357 million doses with options to buy another 152 million more while the EU has secured 1.3 billion with an option for a further 660 million doses.[141]

Mitch McConnell, the majority leader, privately said that he thought voter frustration at the stalemate on the stimulus package could see Georgia's two incumbent Senators toppled if Congress didn't pass a stimulus bill. It is now more than eight months since the first stimulus bill passed into law. But now, with Senators David Perdue and Kelly Loeffler in need of victory before the January 5th run-offs in Georgia, McConnell is pushing forward. Congress' failure to deliver more pandemic assistance would impact Perdue and Loeffler. Draft legislation is now looking at

---

[140] BBC News; Sally Foster: New York Times, Natasha Frost.
[141] New York Times: On Politics.

cheques being sent directly to Americans, which according to Senator John Thune, Republican, should be around $600 to $700 per person although some Democrats are looking for the Spring amount of $1,200 to go out. The bill is expected to include billions of dollars to support vaccine distribution. Hospital pharmacists have found this week that some of the BioNTech distribution is filled with more vaccine than the allotted doses. The Food and Drug Agency said they would authorize use of the extra doses. [142]

It is announced on Thursday 17th December that President Macron of France has tested positive for Coronavirus and is displaying mild symptoms. He is 42 and not in the high-risk category although it is a mystery how he has caught it as he is proudly thought to be very careful, unlike some more cavalier world leaders who have succumbed over the year. Prime Ministers of Spain and Portugal along with others are now self-isolating as they have been in contact with the President. All 27 member countries of the EU prepare to roll out the vaccine programme, beginning on December 27th, 28th and 29th. Also this week King Karl XVI Gustaff of Sweden acknowledges that the country had failed the people with the lockdown resistant model during the pandemic and it has cost 8,000 lives. In the US, as more than 3,600 deaths are announced on Wednesday alone, Vice President Mike Pence and his wife Karen Pence will receive the Pfizer BioNTech vaccine today (18th Dec.) [143]

It is believed Joe Biden will shortly receive the Pfizer-BioNTech vaccine, publicly to demonstrate confidence in the safety of it, along with his wife Jill Biden. Also, likely to be vaccinated is Dr Anthony Fauci, the country's top infectious diseases expert, and Mitch McConnell, the Senate leader and Polio survivor, will also be vaccinated shortly. The first member of Joe Biden's White House staff to test positive for Coronavirus is Representative Cedric Richmond who is now quarantining for 14 days. Biden

---

[142] New York Times: Giovanni Russonello.
[143] New York Times; Daily Brief, Natasha Frost.

names Michael Regan, North Carolina's top environmentalist, to run the Environmental Protection Agency. Regan will be the first black man to run the agency which will tackle climate change and a green-jobs recovery plan. Biden may also appoint Representative Deb Haaland to be his next Secretary of the Interior. She would be the first Native American appointed to the Cabinet Secretary position. Haaland is thought to be an approved pick by progressives and moderates as well as possibly some conservatives. Joe Biden comments for the first time on the investigation into his son Hunter Biden's tax affairs, in an interview with Stephen Colbert on *The Late Show*. He stated he is not concerned and defended Hunter's position. With a stimulus deal suddenly on a fast track some Democrats are worried that Republicans could use it to limit Biden's ability to provide economic relief in the future. In addition to opposing direct aid to state governments, Republicans are seeking to limit the power of the Federal Reserve going forward to extend financing to businesses, municipalities, or other institutions. Democrats say the direct aid to governments is fundamental to keeping public-sector workers employed and the economy stable. [144]

---

[144] The New York Times; Giovanni Russonello.

CHAPTER 44

New Year, New Beginning, New President

A new variant of the virus is discovered in the UK and President Macron decides to close Dover Port and French Borders, halting all freight in and out of France to and from the UK. Other European countries are quick to follow, and chaos ensues. The mutation of the virus is thought to spread faster but is no more dangerous and there is no evidence to suggest the vaccine is any less effective against it. All of this coming just one day after Boris Johnson announces a new tier four lockdown for all of London and huge parts of the country while cancelling the previous five days of restrictions to be eased around Christmas. Christmas is now just one day of allowing up to three households and eight people to meet indoors with the same list of exemptions in place. The First Minister in Scotland follows this directive and goes further by urging everyone to stay home alone in their own household for Christmas. It is thought the variant virus would take years to evolve into a further threat. As Britain reels from the Christmas lockdown, with all of Scotland going into lockdown from midnight on 25th, it perhaps diverts attention from the ongoing Brexit crisis. No deal is ever more likely, and the chaos of the port closure yesterday shows what is about to happen with possible food shortages almost instantly. [145]

Britain continues to rage at its own government as almost 1,000

---

[145] New York Times: Natasha Frost.

lorries remain stranded, parked up on motorways in Kent waiting to cross to France. Many are trying to return to their home countries for Christmas. Travel restrictions form 40 countries, planes, ferries all cancelled. In London, an Australian, living in the UK, said, "The rest of the world looks at us and shakes their heads, it's not very nice to be on a Plague Island and nobody wants you." The tunnel is also hard hit already by the pandemic as more than 90 percent of the employees are furloughed, finances in ruin, and passengers all but vanished. The markets also took a tumble yesterday with the pound falling around 1.8 to the dollar before it recovered slightly.

In other news the much-awaited stimulus package is moving forward as Congress approved the $900 billion bill which will see a $600 payment to millions of Americans who earn up to $75,000. Also, in Delaware, Joe Biden goes public with his Coronavirus vaccine. He has had the Pfizer-BioNTech vaccine, and his wife Jill had hers privately earlier in the day. It is expected that Vice President Kamala Harris will have hers after Christmas so that they have staggered vaccinations, possibly to mitigate any problem if either suffered a reaction. [146]

By the morning of 23rd December France had opened the border to the 1,500 lorries parked on motorways in Kent, England. Some freight will be allowed to cross subject to the driver having a Covid-19 test with negative results. Some 50 countries have blocked UK travel in any form and the EU urges them all to reconsider, but they make their own rules over their own borders. The variant of the virus is already present in Europe, in fact it may have come to England from Europe. Meanwhile, a fresh political crisis in Israel sees the country facing the fourth presidential election in two years. Parliament dissolved itself after failing to agree a new budget by the deadline and an election will now take place on 23rd March 2021. In America, evidence shows that the Russian hackers managed to access the email system of the

---

[146] New York Times: Natasha Frost.

Treasury Department's top leadership, proving how far the invasion had gone into the Trump administration. As Christmas Eve dawns, in the UK Brexit talks have continued overnight and an announcement of a trade deal is expected imminently as last-minute glitches over fishing rights is ironed out. Flights from South Africa are banned to the UK as a second variant of Coronavirus is found in the UK which is believed to have originated from South Africa. The US and Pfizer BioNTech reached a deal for a further 100 million doses of the vaccine which should be available by July. Switzerland begins vaccinating with the Pfizer BioNTech vaccine.[147]

By late afternoon in the UK the Prime Minister announces the Brexit deal is agreed. Last minute compromise on both sides brings the deal the UK wanted, and the EU concedes on a couple of points over fishing rights and trade tariffs. MPs will vote in Parliament on 30th December to approve it and Labour leader Sir Keir Starmer said he will support it. The European Parliament needs to ratify it but will be unlikely to do so before December 31st so it will be a provisional deal but should still mean that the chaos of a no deal is avoided. There are still, however, thousands of lorries stranded at Dover Port and in Kent after the shambles of Macron closing the border, supposedly for 48 hours, on Sunday. Many organisations and volunteers are helping with food, water, toilets, and urgent Covid-19 testing is taking place to allow the drivers to proceed with the journey.[148]

Here in the UK, as Boxing Day begins, all of mainland Scotland enters the highest tier four of restrictions. Essential shopping only as others are now closed, hospitality is closed except for takeaways, gyms are closed. The travel ban permits travel only in our own local council area except for work, to buy medicine, or to care for an elderly or vulnerable person. No indoor visitors are permitted but outdoor contact with one other household up to six

---

[147] New York Times.
[148] BBC News UK.

people is allowed. All close-contact services such as hair and beauty treatments are closed. Cinemas and theatres are closed. Golf courses remain open for play, but clubhouses are closed. Running or walking seems to be all that is left to do in a very small area. Families remain apart. No visits to hospital patients or care home residents permitted. Have we come to accept the emotional pain of this? We have no choice. All is to be reviewed in three weeks. It is mid-Winter, dark nights, cold, and everyone is weary. Pandemic fatigue is becoming very real and as the New Year looms and the Brexit deal to be voted on soon, it remains to be seen what the first week in January looks like. Vaccination rolls out continues and it is hoped that in a few months the impact of this reduces the spread of Coronavirus and maybe by Easter the situation will be better.[149]

Europe begins a campaign to vaccinate more than 450 million people, starting with the elderly and the people who care for them, medical staff, and vulnerable high-risk groups. Many countries are seeing the highest number of cases since the pandemic began. In Britain, a variant of the virus is spreading rapidly and the news of the roll out of a second vaccine in the UK is much anticipated. The Oxford University and AstraZeneca vaccine is easier to distribute and could make a difference to easing lockdown in the UK if the programme gets underway. In the US, as Trump signs the stimulus bill passed by Congress, the figures show that the total number of infections has passed 19 million and more than 330,000 people have died.[150]

On 29th December it is reported that the House voted on Monday evening to increase the size of the stimulus bill, raising the cheques to individuals from $600 to $2,000. Trump demanded it and Senate Republicans were faced with voting for it or defying the President. [151]

---

[149] Sally Foster.
[150] New York Times: BBC News UK.
[151] New York Times: Natasha Frost.

In the UK on 30th December Parliament voted through the EU Brexit deal, the House of Lords agreed it, and it was signed by Boris Johnson and given Royal assent. A done deal, finally. We will see what disruption ensues on 1st January as there is of course a list of changes to paperwork on movement of people and goods. Four years in the making! At the same time Britain became the first country to approve the AstraZeneca Oxford University vaccine which is cheaper and easier to store and administer than others. The roll out of this vaccine begins on Monday 4th January. It is hoped that this will herald a change for the whole world in the battle against Coronavirus. The vaccine roll out in the USA is going a bit slower than was hoped or predicted. So far, 12.4 million doses have been sent out and 2.8 million doses administered. Officials in the States of Colorado and California have confirmed cases of the Coronavirus variant first found in Britain and it apparently spreads faster. [152]

Coronavirus cases in the US as of 31/12/20: 20,216,991.

Deaths: 350,778.

Coronavirus cases in the UK as of 31/12/20: 2,432,888.

Deaths: 72,548.

World cases as of 31/12/20 – 83,193,729.

Deaths: 1,814,921.[153]

The figures above as the year draws to a close are devastating as each death represents a whole family and network of friends who have lost loved ones and are grieving. Many are also living with "long covid" and life-changing, lasting effects of the illness and some are being readmitted to hospital. Much of the UK is in the highest level of restrictions and any New Year "celebration" will be virtual as events and gatherings are all cancelled as we are urged to stay home in our own households and not even meet up outside. And yet, we should perhaps reflect on 2020 and all the

---

[152] New York Times: Natasha Frost.
[153] Multimedia sources.

heartbreak by also remembering the stories of friendship, compassion, and heroism shown by so many from frontline and key workers to communities who have pulled together to help each other and support the vulnerable. We are closer together in shared anguish and trauma, sadness and fear, and the work of the governments and scientists around the world have brought a glimmer of hope that 2021 will grow from the beginnings of the vaccine roll out into better days ahead. In writing my way through this year I have held on to hope even if I did not always believe in it! The United States of America held the most extraordinary Presidential Election through the "Eye of the Storm", the United Kingdom negotiated a Brexit deal with 27 EU member countries as the devolved nations of Scotland, Wales, and Northern Ireland railed against it and the world now waits for better days as vaccinations bring a reduction in virus cases globally and allows us all to go forward. To rebuild, to grow, and to prosper with Joe Biden in the White House and the UK independent from Europe. Russia remains an unknown but always a threat, and China, where all this began, has still not been held to account.[154]

---

[154] Sally Foster: 31/12/2020.

CHAPTER 45

Happy New Year!

A difficult year ends and the new one dawns with muted celebrations around the globe. In Wuhan where this all began, however, they enjoyed boisterous celebrations. President Trump faces the New Year in the knowledge that he was soundly beaten by President-elect Joe Biden and failed the greatest test of his Presidency to handle the Coronavirus Pandemic. The US numbers showed that at the end of the year some 342,577 Americans had died from Covid-19. Yet still he persisted with pouring scorn on those who urge restrictions and help for the American people. He claimed he did not want to take away personal freedom. [155]

For the first time in Trump's presidency, and just as he has only days left in office, the Senate vetoes his $740 billion defense bill. Republicans join with Democrats as Congress rebuffs the bill. The motion to override the bill passed resoundingly at 81-13, a strong bipartisan vote.[156]

Monday 4th brings the revelation that President Trump had a telephone call with Georgia's Republican Secretary of State to find him enough votes to overturn the election result and secure him the electoral college votes. All news agencies carried the story, including the BBC, and it would seem that the President is not going to leave office quietly. House Democrats gave speaker Nancy Pelosi another term in office as the 117th Congress

---

[155] New York Times; Natasha Frost.
[156] Financial Times, Katrina Manson: Washington correspondent.

convened for the first time. With just 222 of 435 votes Ms Pelosi can only afford to lose a few Democrats in any vote. Midnight on Monday in the UK brings a sweeping new stricter lockdown as the new variant of the virus accelerates through all four nations. With freezing temperatures and dark nights, the mood nationwide is sombre but the approval of a second vaccine and the continued roll out of the programme gives a glimmer of hope that by Easter we will all see light at the end of the tunnel. The aim is to suppress the virus until the vaccine roll out does the job for us, to allow an easing of restrictions. [157]

January 6th goes down in history as a sad day for democracy in the United States of America. The first result from the Georgia run-off sees Rev Raphael Warnock topple Kelly Loeffler and become the first black person to hold the position in Georgia. As the race between Jon Osoff and David Perdue looks like a win for Osoff, it seems more and more likely that the Democrats will take control of the Senate. However, before the result is even in and as the debate to confirm Joe Biden as President on electoral college votes, the Capitol Building is stormed by Republican supporters following a Trump rally. Protestors forced their way into the building to stop the counting of the votes. Mike Pence and lawmakers were evacuated. The police, the F.B.I, and then the National Guard fought for three hours during which time the Capitol remained in lockdown until finally control was regained. One woman was shot and later died in hospital. Three more died although it is not clear how. Mike Pence had declared he would not support overturning the election result. Joe Biden called on President Trump to end the violence. Trump appeared and said the election was a fraud but asked protestors to go home and let peace prevail. The rest of the world watched in shock as events unfolded from Washington. Twitter blocked Trump's account after he posted inaccurate and inflammatory tweets and Facebook swiftly followed. Hours after Trump ranted on social media

---

[157] New York Times: Victoria Shannon: BBC News UK.

condoning the violence, White House staff began to resign. Stephanie Grisham being one of the first who was former White House press secretary, Chief of Staff for Melania Trump. The victory in the Georgia runoffs was largely swamped in the mayhem at the Capitol building. Photographs and videos going around the world of the extraordinary scenes inside the building of the National Guard holding weapons over Republican lawmakers and protestors splayed out on the floor of the United States Senate. However, the victory with the thinnest of margins will shape the balance of power in Congress. Trump's single term in office concludes with him losing the Presidency, the House, and the Senate. Unrest in Washington also spread to other states and in Atlanta a mob of protestors led to the evacuation of Secretary of State Brad Raffensberger and some of his staff members. [158]

Condemnation of the President's part in the assault on the Capitol flows in from world leaders today amid calls for him to be impeached, removed from office, and to invoke the 25th amendment. Likely none of these will happen and there is probably not enough time left in office to action anyway but enough to prompt a sombre President Trump to finally voice condemnation of those who broke the law in the storming of the Capitol, praise his supporters, and more vitally finally conceding defeat and offer to focus on a smooth transition of power to a new Administration on the 20th January. Details emerge of those involved in the riots. The woman killed by a gunshot fired by a police officer was a veteran of the air force. The mob also included a newly elected West Virginia lawmaker, white nationalists, conspiracy theorists, and many had travelled from other States to heed the President's call to overturn the election result. Questions are being asked over why it appeared so easy for the white intruders to breach the security and ransack the building and comparisons drawn that if they had been black rioters the

---

[158] New York Times: Daily Brief and On Politics team. Victoria Shannon.

outcome would have been different. [159]

January 8th to 15th

By Monday 11th January, the news is dominated in the US by talk of impeaching President Trump for his part in the violence and attacks on the Capitol building. His term in office expires in a matter of days though and even the fastest ever debate in the Senate would likely not be timely enough. The Senate, however, has the power to remove Trump from office and to prevent him holding any future office. This would shape the future of American politics for sure. The House could vote on Tuesday on the article of impeachment, charging Trump with inciting violence resulting in the attack on the Capitol, but delay sending it to the Senate for trial in order not to tie up Biden's first few days of Presidency. Dozens of people have been arrested and charged for their part in the attack on the Capitol, including one person from QAnon. Trump is now banned from Twitter so has lost a "voice" and now must look for another way to be heard (once out of office).

In other Monday morning news, the new variants of the virus are causing huge concern and muting the hope as the various vaccines are rolled out around the world. It is a race against time to get the elderly, health care workers, care home staff and residents, and the clinically extremely vulnerable vaccinated before hospitals and health care systems are overwhelmed. To show perspective, Dr Anthony Fauci predicts that theatres and other venues may reopen in the fall of 2021 if the vaccine roll out is successful. Other countries, including Britain, have their own targets and predictions.[160] Later on Tuesday night the House passed a resolution calling on Mike Pence and the Cabinet to remove Trump from office although he had already said he would

---

[159] New York Times morning brief by Andrea Kannapell and Melina Delkic.
[160] New York Times, Daily Brief: Natasha Frost.

not do so, and a second impeachment vote is due today, 13th January. Mitch McConnell believes Trump's actions and words before the assault on the Capitol are impeachable offences. Trump shows no remorse and goes further by saying the impeachment talk is causing great anger and frustration. [161]

In the UK, the Covid-19 situation is critical. In London 1 in 30 people are thought to be infected with the virus and further restrictions are expected to be announced in all four nations as the minority are not complying and many breeches will now be more aggressively fined. Hospitals are close to capacity across the UK, and we are all urged to stay at home and only leave for essential purposes; work, medical, care for a vulnerable person, and shopping for food and medicines. [162]

With Nancy Pelosi presiding over proceedings on 13th January, Congress voted 232 to 197 to impeach President Trump, making him the only President to be impeached twice. The charge is "inciting insurrection." The assault on the Capitol last week saw five people die, including one police officer. While a few loyal Republicans defended him, 10 Republicans joined the Democrats in the vote to impeach.[163] As more people are charged in connection with the violence from States far and wide, it became apparent that they were armed and dangerous, angry, and intent on violence. The National Guard protected proceedings yesterday inside and outside Congress, heavily armed and some 20,000 troops are expected on Inauguration Day in Washington. One example in court papers filed on Wednesday in the case of Cleveland G Meredith Jr shows a text message in which he said he wanted to "put a bullet in the noggin of speaker Nancy Pelosi live on TV". [164] Lawmakers are calling for investigation into why visitors were given access to the Capitol the day before as it turned out many were rioters who had been given a guided tour to

---

[161] New York Times, Daily Brief: Natasha Frost.
[162] New York Times, Daily Brief: Natasha Frost. BBC News UK.
[163] New York Times, Daily Brief: Natasha Frost.
[164] New York Times: Alan Feuer, Luke Broadwater.

ease their path of destruction and attack the very next day. Outrage and anger prevails in the mood of Congress. All who enter must pass through metal detectors now. Nancy Pelosi warns of fines for those who don't comply as several Republicans set off the alarms and walked defiantly onto the floor. Some say it is unnecessary, unconstitutional and endangers members. Further saying that metal detectors outside Capitol would not have deterred the rioters of last week and accused Pelosi of a "political stunt." The acting sergeant-at-arms in the House said all people, including lawmakers, must pass through security screening when entering the House Chamber. Failure to comply could result in access being denied. In the same memo it is stated that firearms are "restricted to a member's office." [165]

In other news Aleksei Navalny is due to fly to Moscow this weekend following recovery from the poisoning even though he is likely to be arrested on arrival. It is his home, and he is resolute in returning. The WHO finally arrive in Wuhan after months of wrangling to investigate the origin of the Coronavirus. Scottish Seafood businesses are being severely disrupted by Brexit paperwork and regulations. Calls to the government for help amid the reality of boats lying idle, fish rotting, and families suffering hardship.[166] The 15th dawns with news from the US of Biden's plan for a $1.9 trillion rescue package. It is thought $400 billion is to directly tackle the issues of the pandemic and $350 billion for state and local government budget shortfalls. 1.5 million workers filed for state unemployment benefits last week. A further 284,000 workers filed for emergency federal support from a group which includes freelance and part-time workers. Both figures are the highest in months. Inauguration planning sees thousands of National Guards arrive in Washington to prepare for the most unusual inauguration ceremony as the F.B.I urges all State police chiefs to be on alert for extremist activity. Trump, meanwhile, is about to face trial in the Senate over impeachment charges. If

---

[165] New York Times: Michael Levenson and Emily Cochrane.
[166] New York Times; Daily Brief.

convicted he will not hold public office again. [167]

Joe Biden, while not progressives' first choice, looks to be preparing to "go big" with the announcement of the $1.3 trillion economic rescue package. With Democratic control of both Houses, he will push an aggressive economic agenda without holding back as is more typical of moderate Democrats. Areas of concern highlighted in the package include "infrastructure, manufacturing, innovation, research and development, and clean energy." He indicated the plans will increase employment, tackle poverty and stimulate business growth, and bring down the deficit, but in discussing the pandemic and other issues he put economic justice at the heart. He promises investment in America, in American goods, in the American people. Biden also spoke of the dismal failure of the vaccine roll out so far and will "move heaven and earth to get more people vaccinated." The $400 billion allocated from the economic rescue package will help coordinate the circulation of vaccines, increase funding for testing, and buy more personal protective equipment. With slim majorities, however, in both Houses, Biden will face an uphill battle in delivering plans. Prominent Republicans already fired back on social media that it is too fast and too much! And the outcome of the trial of President Trump will either quieten him or allow him to continue filibustering. [168]

January 16th to 19th

By way of a short summary, as Trump prepares to depart from the White House, we know that after four years in office where he bullied rivals, intimidated his enemies, flooded social media with misinformation, and you could say "abused" his command of the world stage, the President leaves having been snubbed by foreign

---

[167] New York Times, Daily Brief: Natasha Frost.
[168] New York Times: Giovanni Russonello.

allies and banned from social media while becoming the only United States President to be impeached twice and as we all know is facing trial in the Senate. Having arrived as an insurgent and unlikely President, he leaves isolated and diminished in the wake of the violent extraordinary attacks on the Capitol just days before Joe Biden's inauguration. (The assault on the Capitol seems to have been pre-planned for months across States and claimed that security forces and Congress were aware). While outgoing presidents have thrived post presidency with varying ventures, from George W Bush painting to Barack Obama writing books and making speeches, what next for President Trump? A true pariah? It is known he will not attend the inauguration and further that he plans to leave Washington hours before President-elect Joe Biden is sworn in, making him the first President to skip inauguration of his successor since Andrew Johnson in 1869 who was also impeached. Will he flee to Mar-a-lago in Florida? His resorts and hotels are just as affected by the pandemic as others suffering across the hospitality industry. Added to his personal financial woes and the position regarding the hosting of major golf tournaments at his golf courses taken by the USPGA and several other governing bodies in golf he has lots of hurdles. Yet, no doubt he will be heard and not adopt the policy of keeping a low profile as he loves the limelight. Also, he has a trial to face. [169]

Inauguration Day: Washington Prepares

Firstly, Washington prepares for unrest and urges people not to attend in person due to the ongoing pandemic so a virtual inauguration will set a precedent.

Mr Biden will be sworn in before 12 noon by Chief Justice John G Roberts on the Capitol's West Front. Then, as is tradition, the new President will give his inaugural address and inspect troops. Lady

---

[169] New York Times: On Politics: Lisa Lerer.

Gaga will sing the National Anthem and Jennifer Lopez will give a musical performance. There will be no traditional parade in front of spectators, rather the President, Vice President, and their families will make their way along Pennsylvania Avenue to the White House, a mile away, with an official escort with representatives of every military branch for one city block. [170]

Aleksei Navalny returns to Moscow on Sunday 17th January, five months after being poisoned (it is thought by Russian agents) with nerve agent Novichok. Flying from Germany to Moscow, the flight was diverted from Vnukovo airport where supporters had gathered to Sheremetyevo, for "technical reason", and Mr Navalny was detained instantly on arrival and led away after saying goodbye to his wife. The US and European Governments condemn the Russian forces' actions and call for his release. Russia's Foreign Minister dismissed the West's protest as being "a way to divert interest from domestic problems." Mr Navalny is 44 years of age and is the most prominent opposition to President Putin. Russia's prison service said Mr Navalny has violated the terms of his suspended sentence for embezzlement and will remain in custody until a court ruling. [171]

With Tuesday 19th January being President Trump's last full day in office, and as I anticipate tomorrow's historic Inauguration Ceremony, I take just a moment to reflect before recording the press reports from the New York Times *this morning from my inbox. When I began this process I never thought for one moment back in February 2020 that the journey would lead anywhere but to a normal process of Democratic Primaries (which is what I wanted to focus on!) followed by an orderly Presidential election and a new President or a second term for Donald Trump. What began as indulging my interest in American Politics became a fascinating, heart-breaking, challenging, and, at times, exhausting commitment to record a period of history not just in America, but*

---

[170] New York Times: Morning Politics: Aishvarya Kavi.
[171] BBC News.

here in the UK and indeed around the world. Daily news reports from the truly inspiring team at the New York Times, hours of pouring through facts and figures, statistics, and science, recording the Primary results, tracking the economy, social and racial injustices, employment, to name some areas of interest. Added to that I included Brexit, China and the WHO investigation, Russia, and their on-going Cyber interference. The pandemic is a subject all of its own. The content just grew and while trying to stay on task it became impossible to just look at the presidential election as it was dominated by all of the above factors and, as President-elect Joe Biden prepares to take office tomorrow, there are many news strands to record. I always intended to finish with the inauguration speech, so I will. However, I will continue to read every report, follow the new President's journey, the fortunes of America, my home nation, and of course the pandemic, vaccine roll out, and one day soon a gradual return to less restrictions and, like President Biden, New Beginnings! [172]

Joe Biden prepares to take office and plans a 10-day blitz of executive orders to tackle some of Trump's more controversial policies. Also, he will begin to reverse some of President Trump's legacy by likely reversing the travel ban on several predominantly Muslim countries, re-joining the Paris climate change accord, and extending pandemic-related limits on evictions and student loan payments. The incoming Vice President Kamala Harris will today resign from her Senate seat before being sworn in tomorrow. Military vehicles and police barricades line the streets near government buildings as officials brace for the influx of Trump supporters and possible violence. [173]

---

[172] Sally Foster.
[173] New York Times: Daily Brief: Giovanni Russonello.

New Beginnings – Inauguration Day, January 20th 2021

"This is Democracy's Day"

Joseph Robinette Biden is sworn in as the 46th President of the United States of America.

Kamala Harris is sworn in as the first woman, first woman of colour, and first African/South Asian person as Vice President of the United States of America.

Using a five-inch-thick Bible, which has been in his family for 128 years, Joe Biden took the 35-word oath, presided over by Chief Justice John Roberts. The new President began his inaugural speech hailing Democracy, calling for all Americans to put aside bitter differences, and pledging to be a President for "all Americans." After the speeches, the goodbyes, the motorcade, and walk to the White House, President Biden immediately got to work. First up he signed 17 executive orders, memorandums, and proclamations from his seat at his desk in the Oval Office, undoing Trump's policies. He swiftly brought America back in the World Health Organisation and the Paris Climate change accord. Kamala Harris is now the highest-ranking female in American history and could find herself casting the tie-breaking vote in the Senate on crucial pieces of legislation. [174]

As I watched the news special from the BBC in Scotland covering the Inauguration Ceremony with my family, I was acutely aware of the historic events unfolding. On a beautiful, bright, but cold morning in Washington, the streets were subdued. Cordoned off for several blocks by National Guard, police, and security in anticipation of trouble. Socially distanced seating set out for those who could attend. As the former Presidents and First Ladies arrived for the ceremony in masks and gloves, no handshakes were given, marking the presence and the effects of the

---

[174] New York Times: Daily Brief: Natasha Frost.

pandemic. George and Laura Bush, Bill and Hillary Clinton, Barack and Michelle Obama taking their seats in order of terms served with the undeniable air of stature and good manners befitting their place in American history, in stark contrast to the outgoing President. Almost sombre at times in respect of the 400,00 plus Americans who have died of Covid-19. The absence of the outgoing President Trump. His arrival in Florida beaming around the world as Vice President Mike Pence attended the Inauguration in his place with dignity. There was a calmness and yet a promise of a new beginning for America and her people. Of hope for unity for a fractured country. Most of all, perhaps, I was not alone in feeling relief that President Donald Trump has left the White House. As Inauguration Day draws to a close, so too does my daily study. Almost one year of daily reading, writing, researching. This is of course only the beginning for President Biden, and I am looking forward to what's next."

Inauguration speech.

Chief Justice Roberts, Vice-President Harris, Speaker Pelosi, Leader Schumer, Leader McConnell, Vice-President Pence. My distinguished guests, my fellow Americans.

This is America's day. This is democracy's day. A day of history and hope, of renewal and resolve. Through a crucible for the ages, America has been tested anew and America has risen to the challenge. Today we celebrate the triumph not of a candidate but of a cause, a cause of democracy. The people – the will of the people – has been heard, and the will of the people has been heeded.

We've learned again that democracy is precious, democracy is fragile, and, at this hour, my friends, democracy has prevailed. So now on this hallowed ground where just a few days ago violence sought to shake the Capitol's very foundations, we come together as one nation under God – indivisible – to carry out the peaceful transfer of power as we have for more than two centuries.

As we look ahead in our uniquely American way, restless, bold, optimistic, and set our sights on a nation we know we can be and must be, I thank my predecessors of both parties. I thank them from the bottom of my heart. And I know the resilience of our Constitution and the strength, the strength of our nation, as does President Carter, who I spoke with last night who cannot be with us today, but who we salute for his lifetime of service.

I've just taken a sacred oath each of those patriots have taken. The oath first sworn by George Washington. But the American story depends not on any one of us, not on some of us, but on all of us. On we the people who seek a more perfect union. This is a great nation; we are good people. And over the centuries, through storm and strife, in peace and in war, we've come so far. But we still have far to go.

We'll press forward with speed and urgency for we have much to do in this winter of peril and significant possibility. Much to do, much to heal, much to restore, much to build, and much to gain. Few people in our nation's history have been more challenged or found a time more challenging or difficult than the time we're in now. A once-in-a-century virus that silently stalks the country has taken as many lives in one year as in all of World War Two.

Millions of jobs have been lost. Hundreds of thousands of businesses closed. A cry for racial justice, some 400 years in the making, moves us. The dream of justice for all will be deferred no longer. A cry for survival comes from the planet itself, a cry that can't be any more desperate or any more clear now. The rise of political extremism, white supremacy, domestic terrorism, that we must confront, and we will defeat.

To overcome these challenges, to restore the soul and secure the future of America, requires so much more than words. It requires the most elusive of all things in a democracy – unity. Unity. In another January on New Year's Day in 1863 Abraham Lincoln signed the Emancipation Proclamation. When he put pen to paper the president said, and I quote, 'if my name ever goes down in history, it'll be for this act, and my whole soul is in it'.

My whole soul is in it today, on this January day. My whole soul is in this. Bringing America together, uniting our people, uniting our nation. And I ask every American to join me in this cause. Uniting to fight the foes we face – anger, resentment, and hatred. Extremism, lawlessness, violence, disease, joblessness, and hopelessness.

With unity we can do great things, important things. We can right wrongs, we can put people to work in good jobs, we can teach our children in safe schools. We can overcome the deadly virus, we can rebuild work, we can rebuild the middle class and make work secure, we can secure racial justice and we can make America once again the leading force for good in the world.

I know speaking of unity can sound to some like a foolish fantasy these days. I know the forces that divide us are deep and they are real. But I also know they are not new. Our history has been a constant struggle between the American ideal, that we are all created equal, and the harsh ugly reality that racism, nativism, and fear have torn us apart. The battle is perennial, and victory is never secure.

Through civil war, the Great Depression, World War, 9/11, through struggle, sacrifice, and setback, our better angels have always prevailed. In each of our moments enough of us have come together to carry all of us forward and we can do that now. History, faith, and reason show the way. The way of unity.

We can see each other not as adversaries but as neighbours. We can treat each other with dignity and respect. We can join forces, stop the shouting, and lower the temperature. For without unity there is no peace, only bitterness and fury, no progress, only exhausting outrage. No nation, only a state of chaos. This is our historic moment of crisis and challenge. And unity is the path forward. And we must meet this moment as the United States of America.

If we do that, I guarantee we will not fail. We have never, ever, ever, ever failed in America when we've acted together. And so today at this time, in this place, let's start afresh, all of us. Let's begin to listen to one another again, hear one another, see one another. Show respect to one another. Politics doesn't have to be a raging fire destroying everything in its path. Every disagreement doesn't have to be a cause for total war, and we must reject the culture in which facts themselves are manipulated and even manufactured.

My fellow Americans, we have to be different than this. We have to be better than this and I believe America is so much better than this. Just look around. Here we stand in the shadow of the Capitol dome. As mentioned earlier, completed in the shadow of the Civil War. When the union itself was literally hanging in the balance. We endure, we prevail. Here we stand, looking out on the great Mall, where Dr King spoke of his dream.

Here we stand, where 108 years ago at another inaugural, thousands of protesters tried to block brave women marching for the right to vote. And today we mark the swearing in of the first woman elected to national office, Vice President Kamala Harris. Don't tell me things can't change. Here we stand where heroes who gave the last full measure of devotion rest in eternal peace.

And here we stand just days after a riotous mob thought they could use violence to silence the will of the people, to stop the work of our democracy, to drive us from this sacred ground. It did not happen, it will never happen, not today, not tomorrow, not ever. Not ever. To all those who supported our campaign, I'm humbled by the faith you placed in us. To all those who did not support us, let me say this. Hear us out as we move forward. Take a measure of me and my heart.

If you still disagree, so be it. That's democracy. That's America. The right to dissent peacefully. And the guardrail of our democracy is perhaps our nation's greatest strength. If you hear me clearly, disagreement must not lead to disunion. And I pledge this to you. I will be a President for all Americans, all Americans. And I promise you I will fight for those who did not support me as for those who did.

Many centuries ago, St Augustine – the saint of my church – wrote that a people was a multitude defined by the common objects of their love. Defined by the common objects of their love. What are the common objects we as Americans love, that define us as Americans? I think we know. Opportunity, security, liberty, dignity, respect, honour, and yes, the truth.

Recent weeks and months have taught us a painful lesson. There is truth and there are lies. Lies told for power and for profit. And each of us has a duty and a responsibility as citizens, as Americans, and especially as leaders. Leaders who are pledged to honour our Constitution to protect our nation. To defend the truth and defeat the lies.

Look, I understand that many of my fellow Americans view the future with fear and trepidation. I understand they worry about their jobs. I understand, like their dad, they lay in bed at night staring at the ceiling, thinking: 'Can I keep my healthcare? Can I pay my mortgage?' Thinking about their families, about what comes next. I promise you; I get it. But the answer's not to turn inward. To retreat into competing factions. Distrusting those who don't look like you, or worship the way you do, who don't get their news from the same source as you do.

We must end this uncivil war that pits red against blue, rural versus urban, conservative versus liberal. We can do this if we open our souls instead of hardening our hearts, if we show a little tolerance and humility, and if we're willing to stand in the other person's shoes, as my mom would say. Just for a moment, stand in their shoes.

Because here's the thing about life. There's no accounting for what fate will deal you. Some days you need a hand. There are other days when we're called to lend a hand. That's how it has to be, that's what we do for one another. And if we are that way our country will be stronger, more prosperous, more ready for the future. And we can still disagree.

My fellow Americans, in the work ahead of us we're going to need each other. We need all our strength to persevere through this *dark winter. We're entering what may be the darkest and deadliest period of the virus. We must set aside politics and finally face this pandemic as one nation, one nation. And I promise this, as the Bible says, 'Weeping may endure for a night, joy cometh in the morning'. We will get through this together. Together.*

Look folks, all my colleagues I serve with in the House and the Senate up here, we all understand the world is watching. Watching all of us today. So, here's my message to those beyond our borders. America has been tested and we've come out stronger for it. We will repair our alliances and engage with the world once again. Not to meet yesterday's challenges but today's and tomorrow's challenges. And we'll lead not merely by the example of our power but the power of our example.

Fellow Americans, moms, dads, sons, daughters, friends, neighbours, and co-workers. We will honour them by becoming the people and the nation we can and should be. So, I ask you, let's say a silent prayer for those who lost their lives, those left behind, and for our country. Amen.

Folks, it's a time of testing. We face an attack on our democracy, and on truth, a raging virus, a stinging inequity, systemic racism, a climate in crisis, America's role in the world. Any one of these would be enough to challenge us in profound ways. But the fact is we face them all at once, presenting this nation with one of the greatest responsibilities we've had. Now we're going to be tested. Are we going to step up?

It's time for boldness for there is so much to do. And this is certain, I promise you. We will be judged, you and I, by how we resolve these cascading crises of our era. We will rise to the occasion. Will we master this rare and difficult hour? Will we meet our obligations and pass along a new and better world to our children? I believe we must and I'm sure you do as well. I believe we will, and when we do, we'll write the next great chapter in the history of the United States of America. The American story.

A story that might sound like a song that means a lot to me; it's called American Anthem. *And there's one verse that stands out, at least for me, and it goes like this:*

'The work and prayers of centuries have brought us to this day, which shall be our legacy, what will our children say?

Let me know in my heart when my days are through, America, America, I gave my best to you.'

Let us add our own work and prayers to the unfolding story of our great nation. If we do this, then when our days are through, our children and our children's children will say of us: 'They gave their best, they did their duty, they healed a broken land.'

My fellow Americans, I close the day where I began, with a sacred oath. Before God and all of you, I give you my word. I will always level with you. I will defend the Constitution; I'll defend our democracy.

I'll defend America and I will give all – all of you – keep everything I do in your service. Thinking not of power but of possibilities. Not of personal interest but of public good.

And together we will write an American story of hope, not fear. Of unity not division, of light not darkness. A story of decency and dignity, love and healing, greatness, and goodness. May this be the story that guides us. The story that inspires us. And the story that tells ages yet to come that we answered the call of history, we met the moment. Democracy and hope, truth, and justice, did not die on our watch but thrive.

That America secured liberty at home and stood once again as a beacon to the world. That is what we owe our forbearers, one another, and generations to follow.

So, with purpose and resolve, we turn to those tasks of our time. Sustained by faith, driven by conviction, and devoted to one another and the country we love with all our hearts. May God bless America and God protect our troops.

About the Author

Learning through the pen or, in this digital age, through technology where global communication is almost instant brings the world to wherever we live and work from. Inspired by my natural thirst for knowledge, I write from Poetry to Politics from my home in Scotland. We are living through unprecedented times and I continue to learn and grow from the world around me.

Printed in Great Britain
by Amazon